THIS BOOK
BELONGS TO:

_ _ _ _ _ _ _ _ _ _ _ _

Dedicated to all my friends and family who 'came' along on this journey with me! Love y'all!

Check us out on our socials!

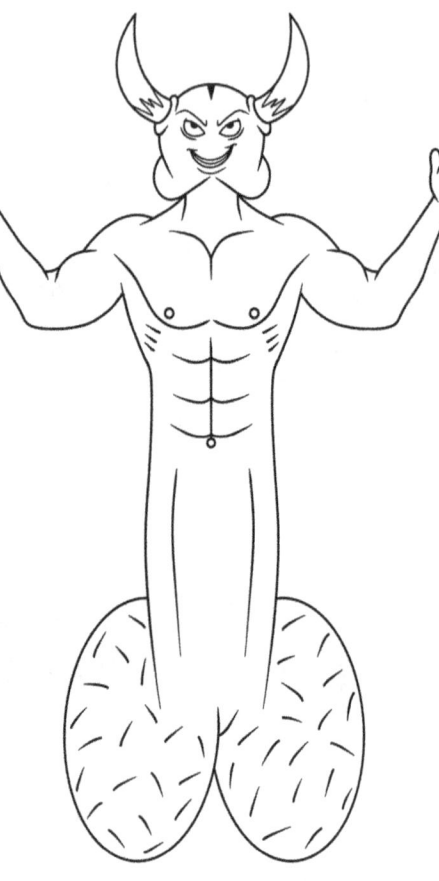

Facebook
@MarcusLongfellaProductions

Instagram
@MarcusLongfellaProductions

Twitter
@MarcusLongfella

TikTok
@MarcusLongfella

Don't be a dick and leave us a review on Amazon!

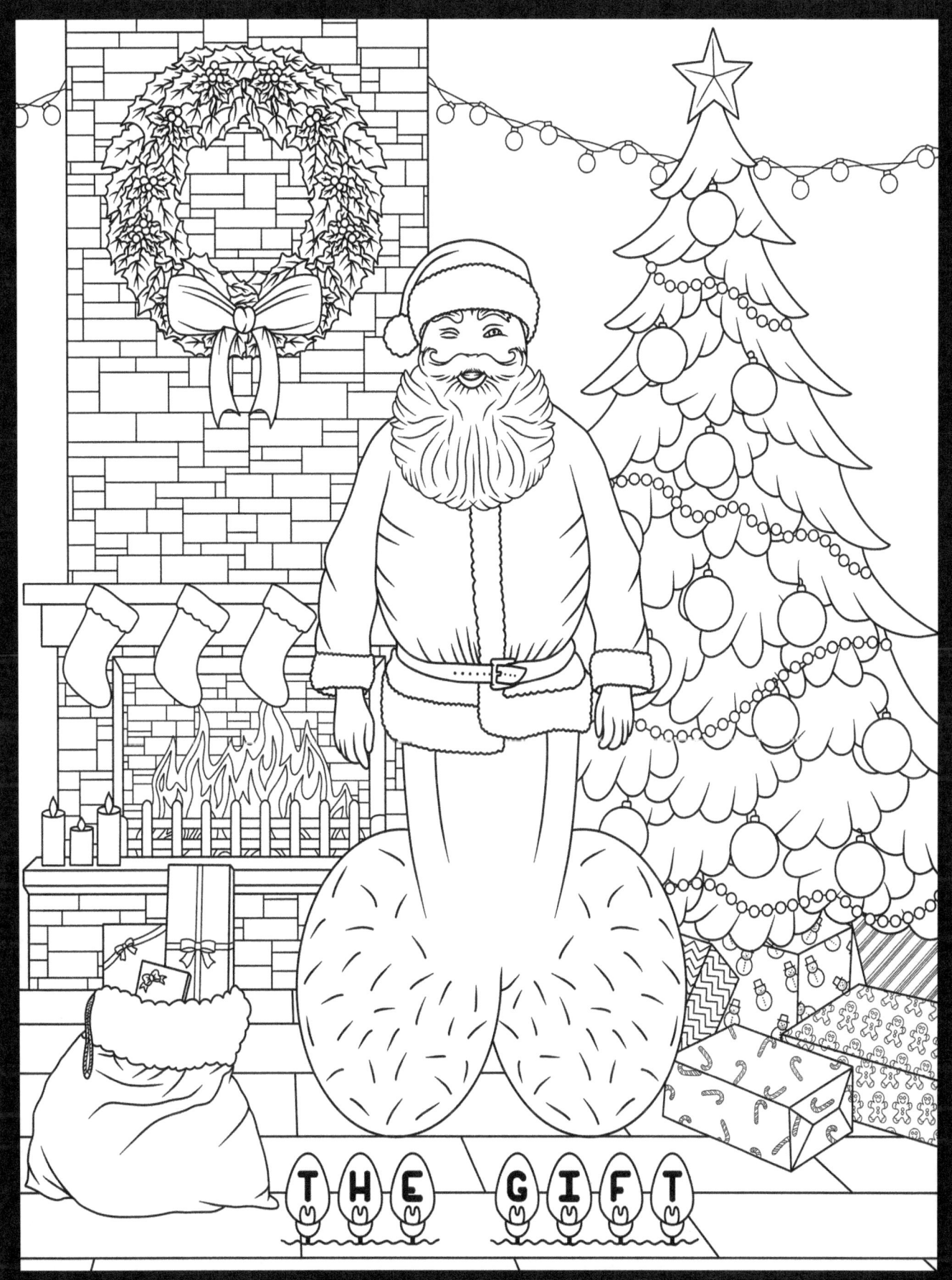

THE GIFT

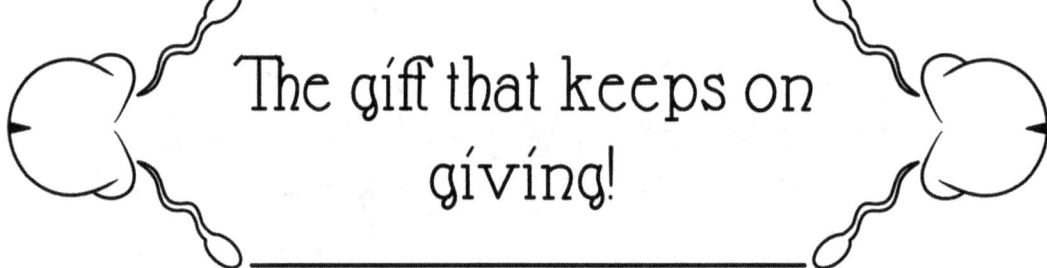

The gift that keeps on giving!

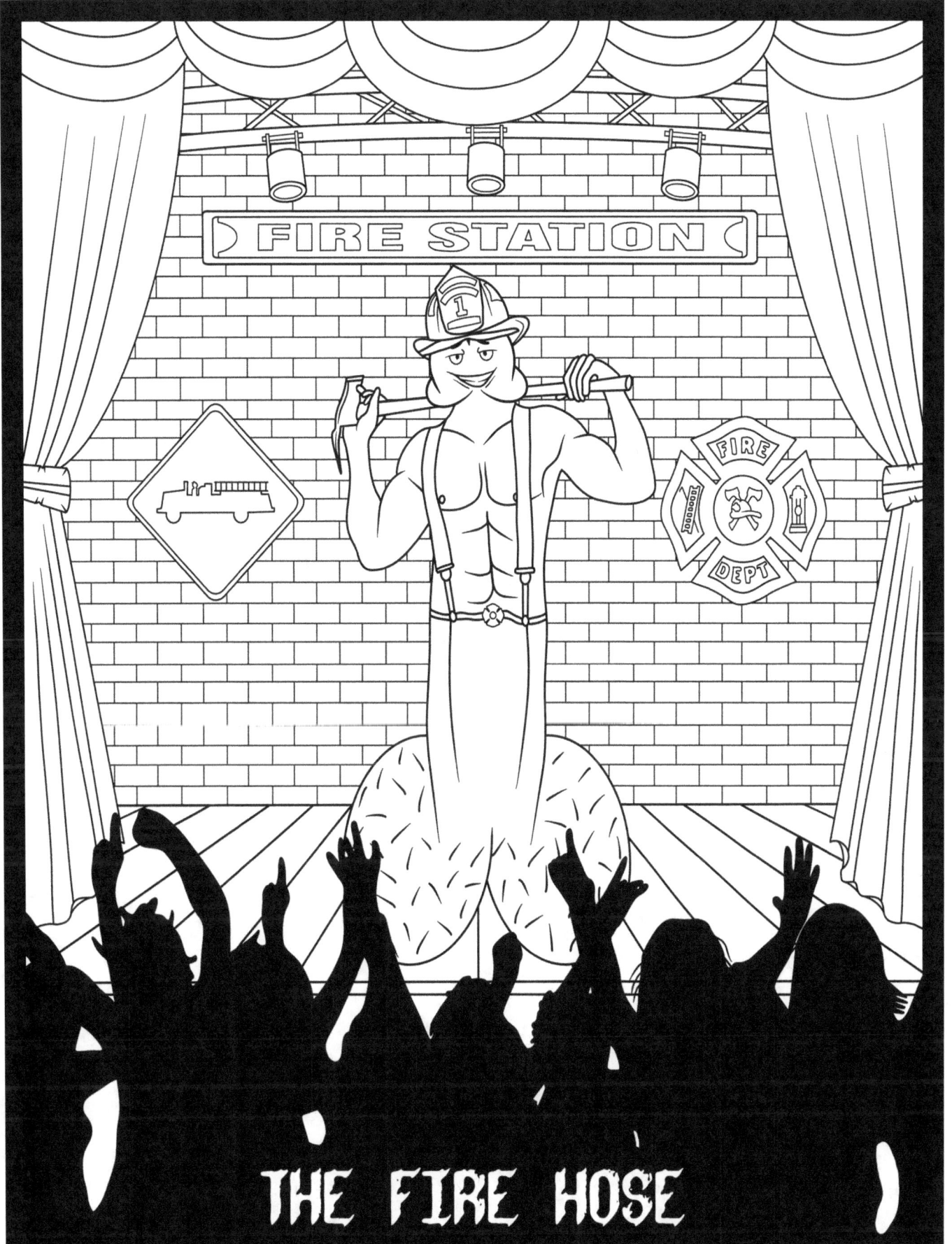

When storylines mean
nothing, but you need
to put that fire out!

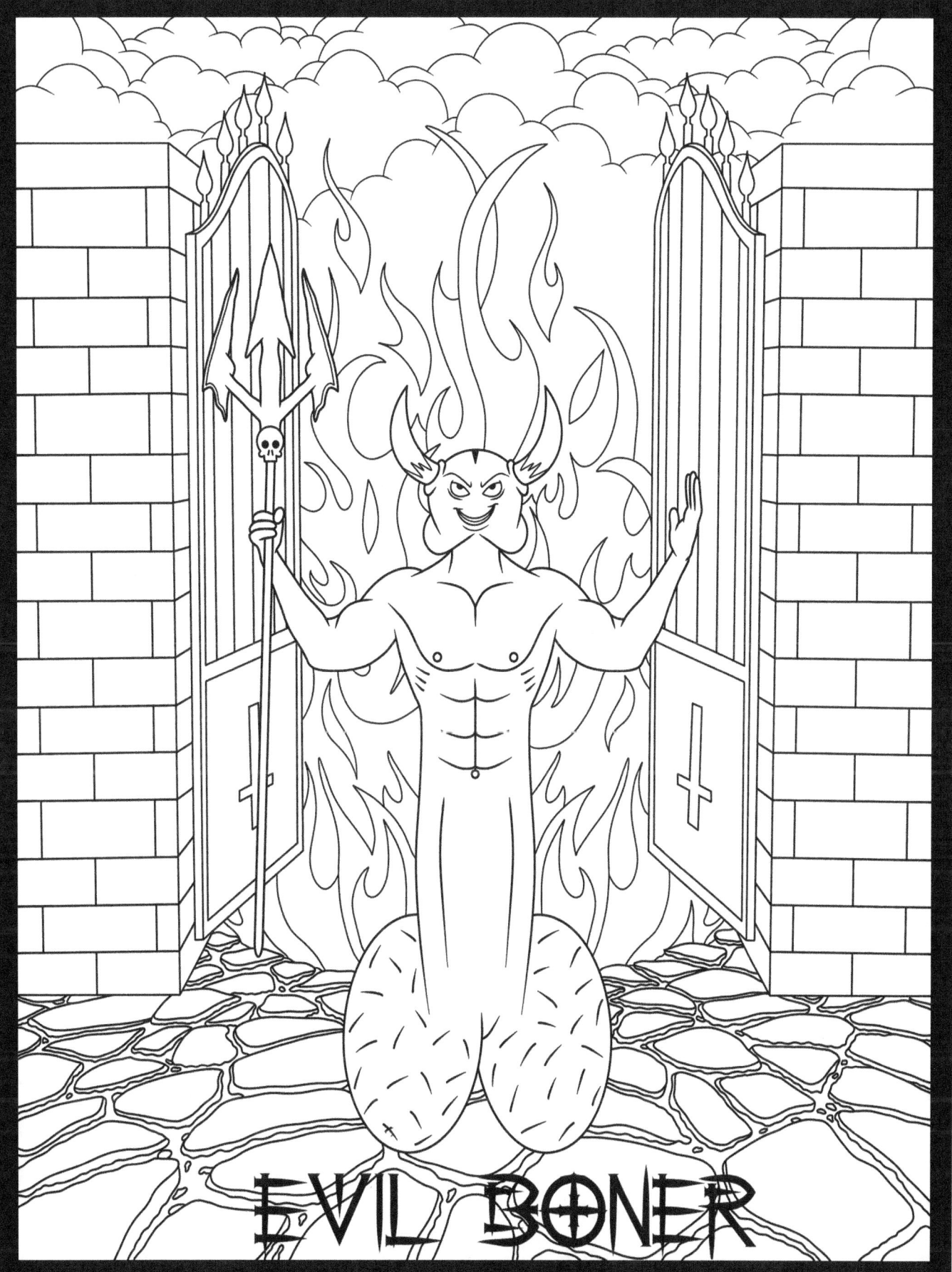

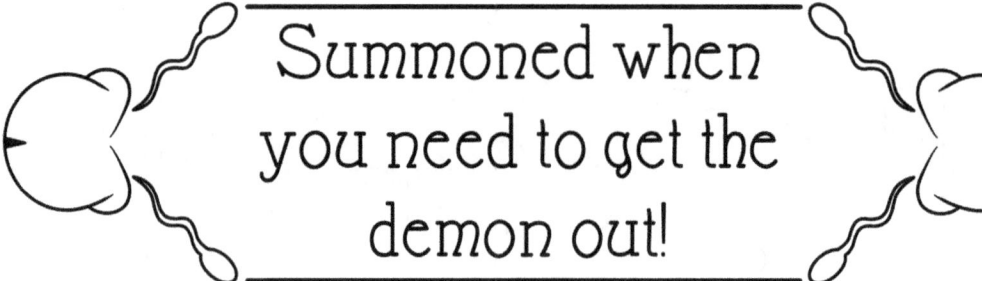

Summoned when
you need to get the
demon out!

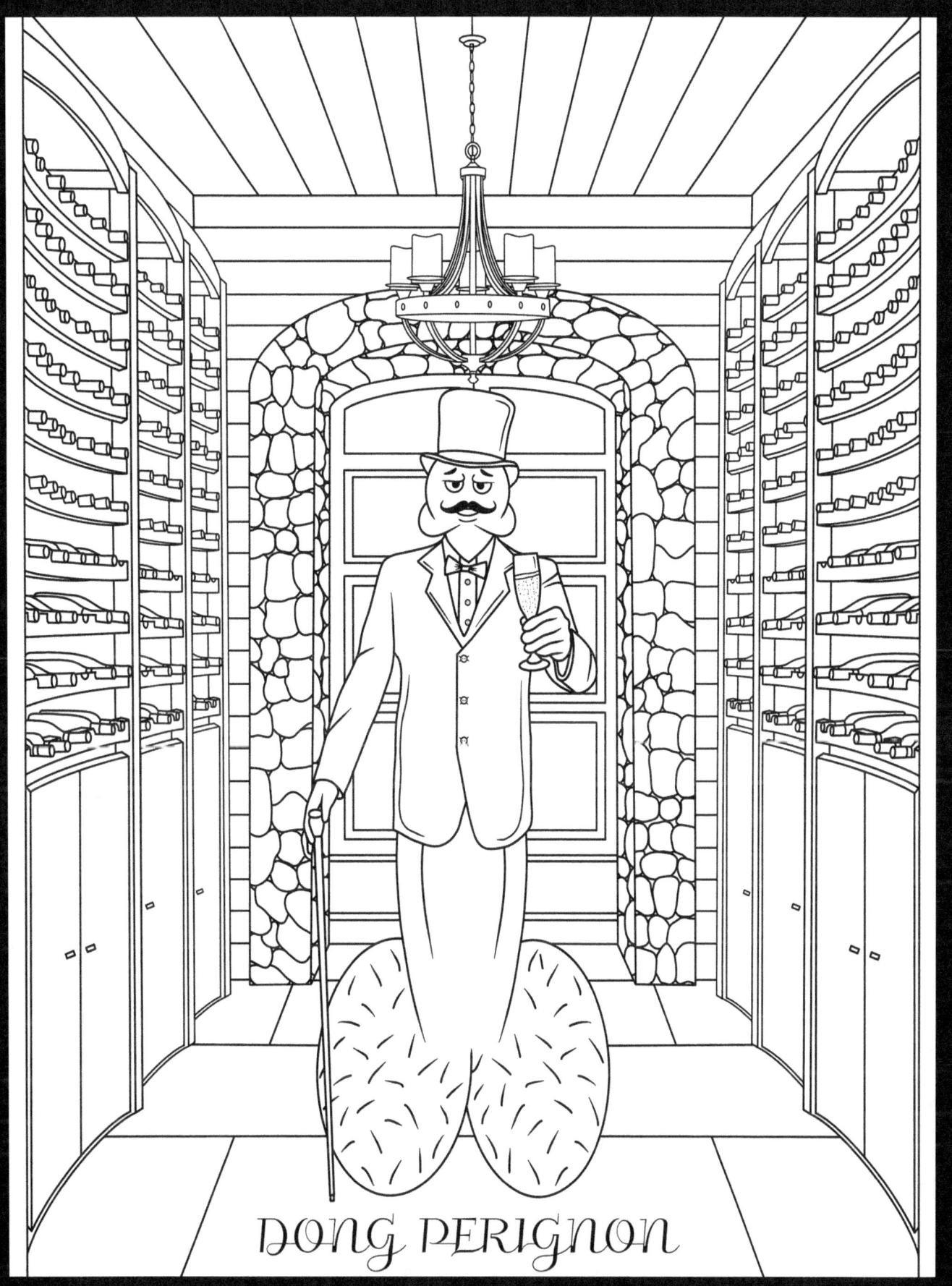

DONG PERIGNON

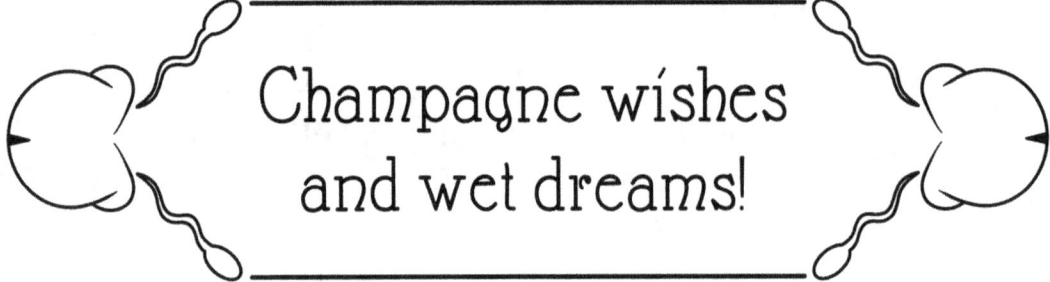

Champagne wishes
and wet dreams!

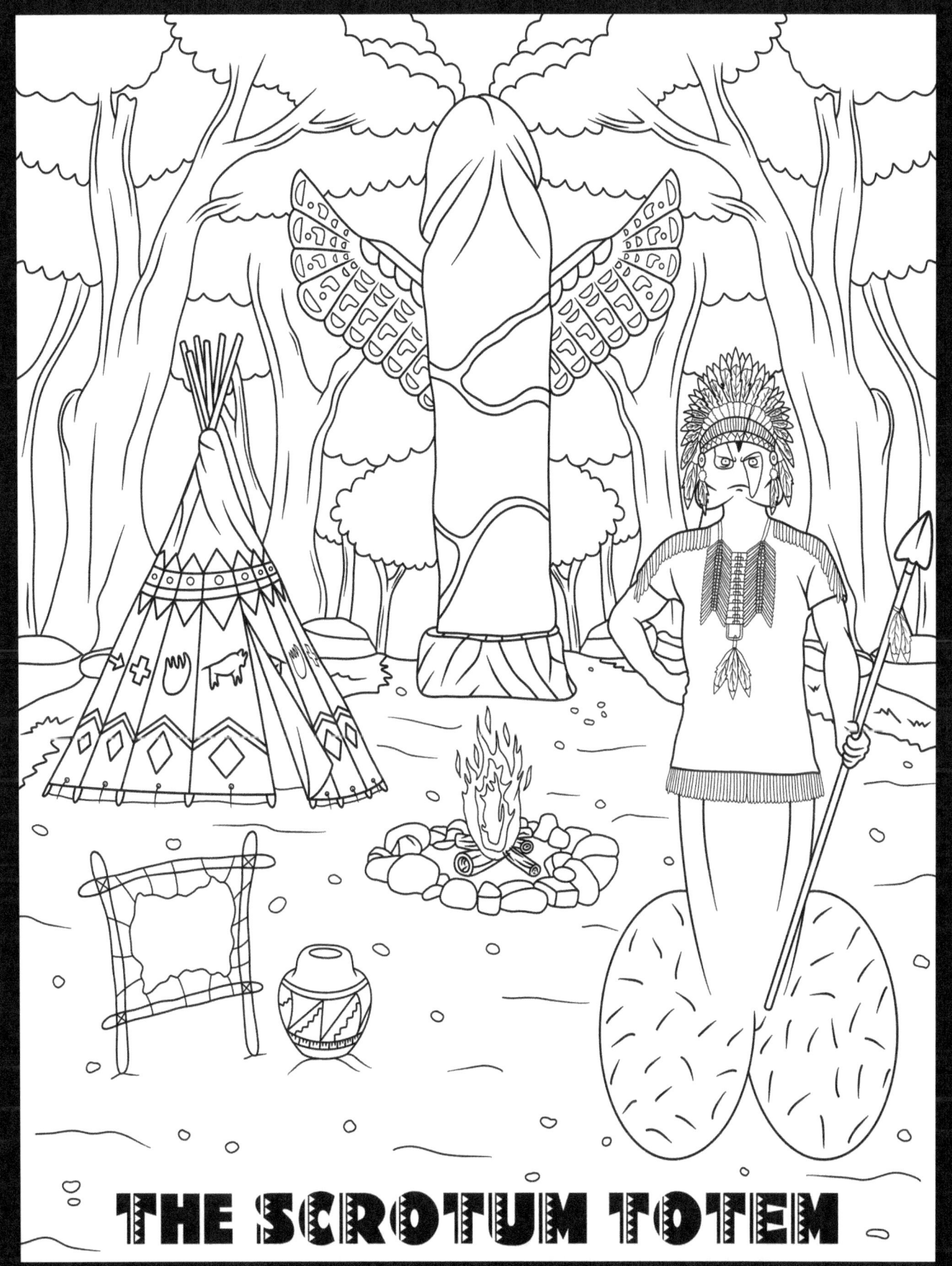

THE SCROTUM TOTEM

When you want to bring
out her spirit animal!

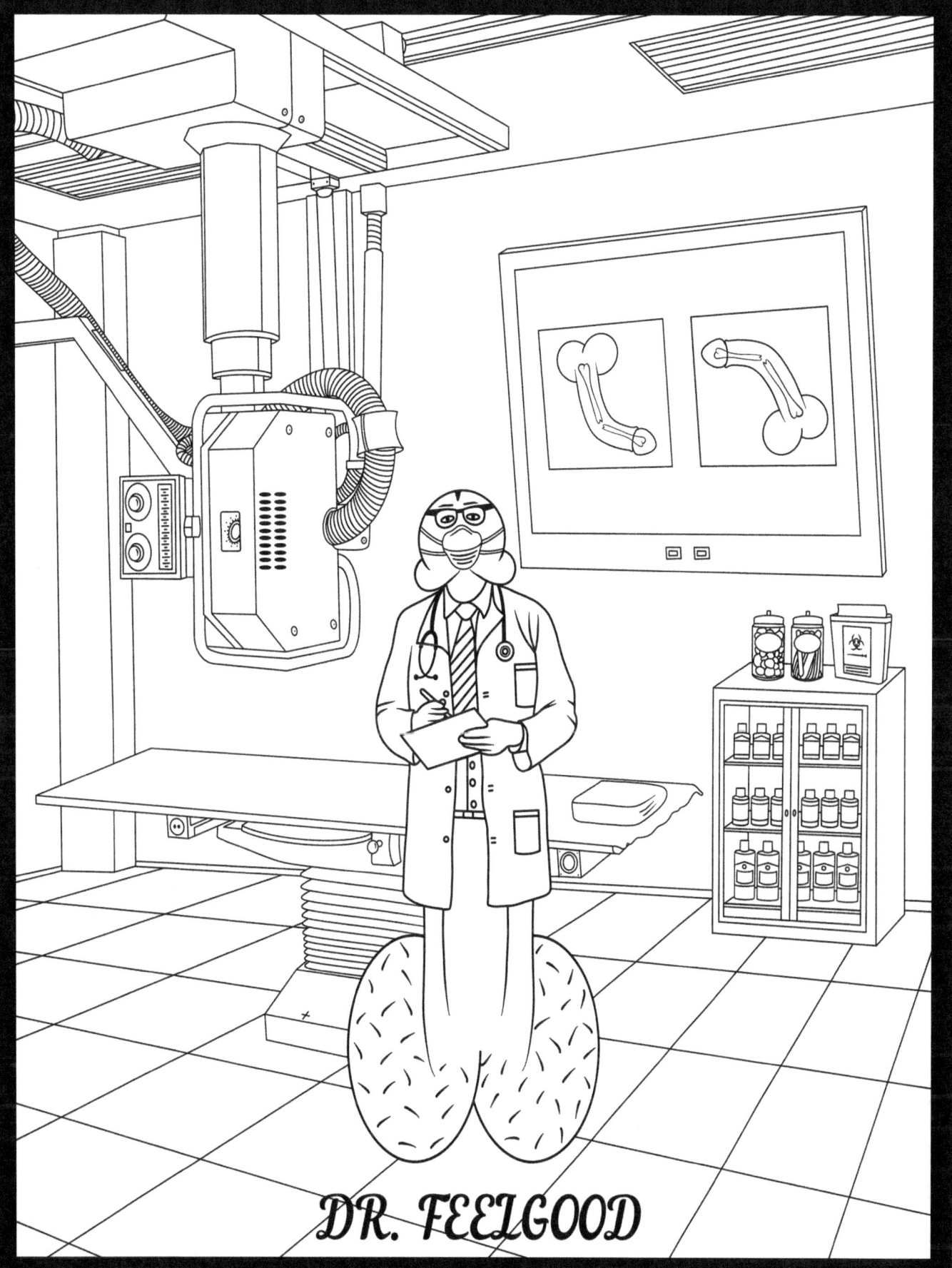

DR. FEELGOOD

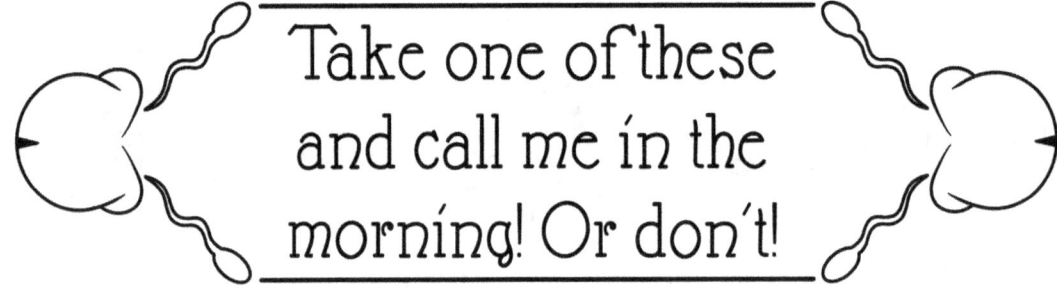

Take one of these and call me in the morning! Or don't!

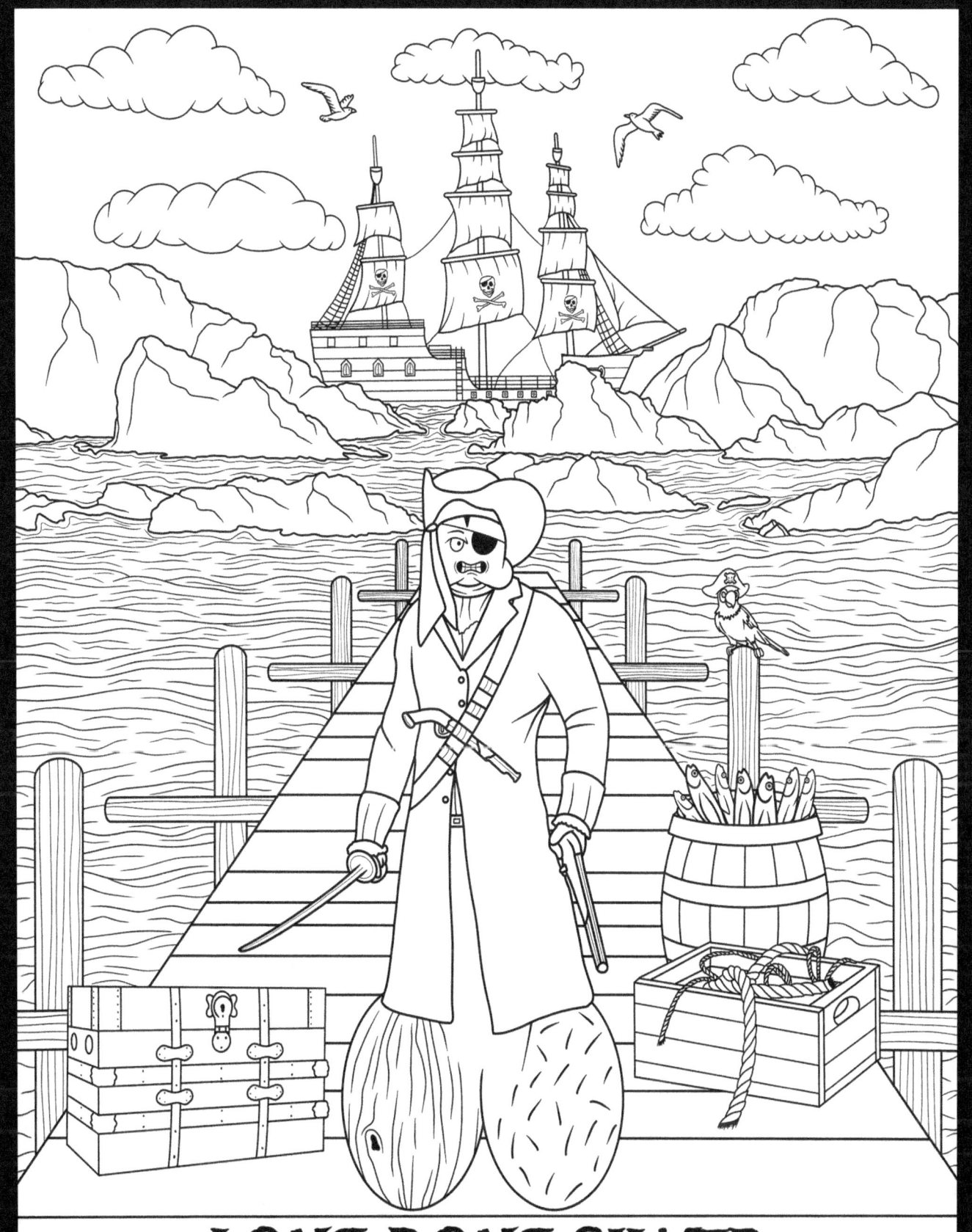

LONG DONG SILVER

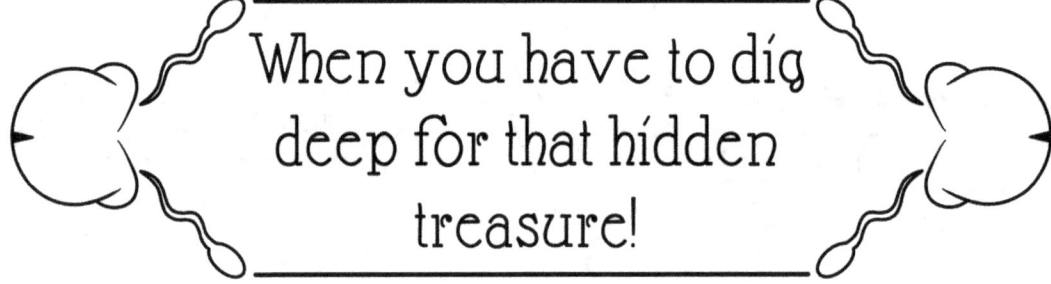

When you have to dig
deep for that hidden
treasure!

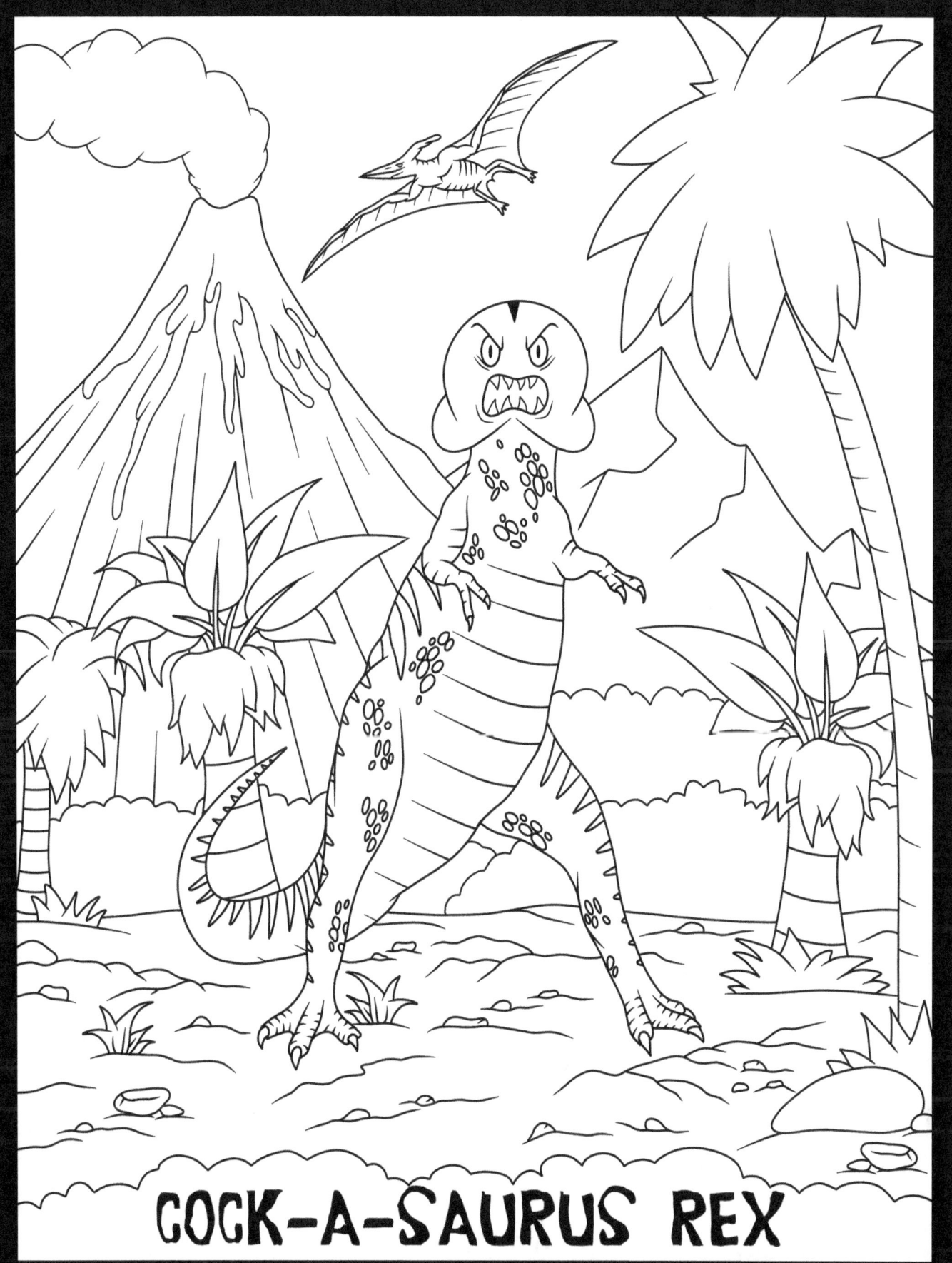

COCK-A-SAURUS REX

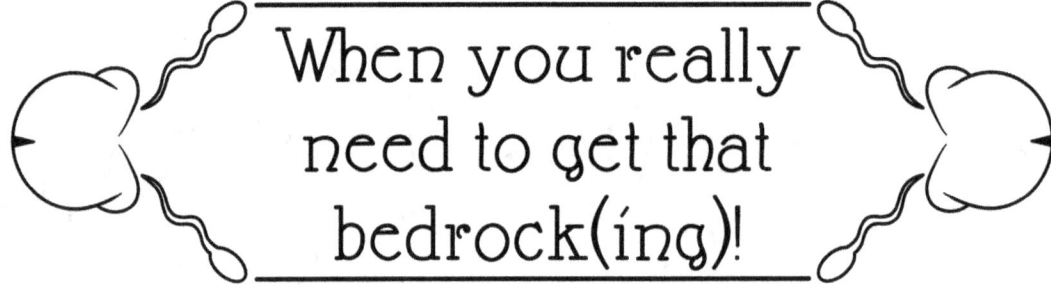

When you really
need to get that
bedrock(ing)!

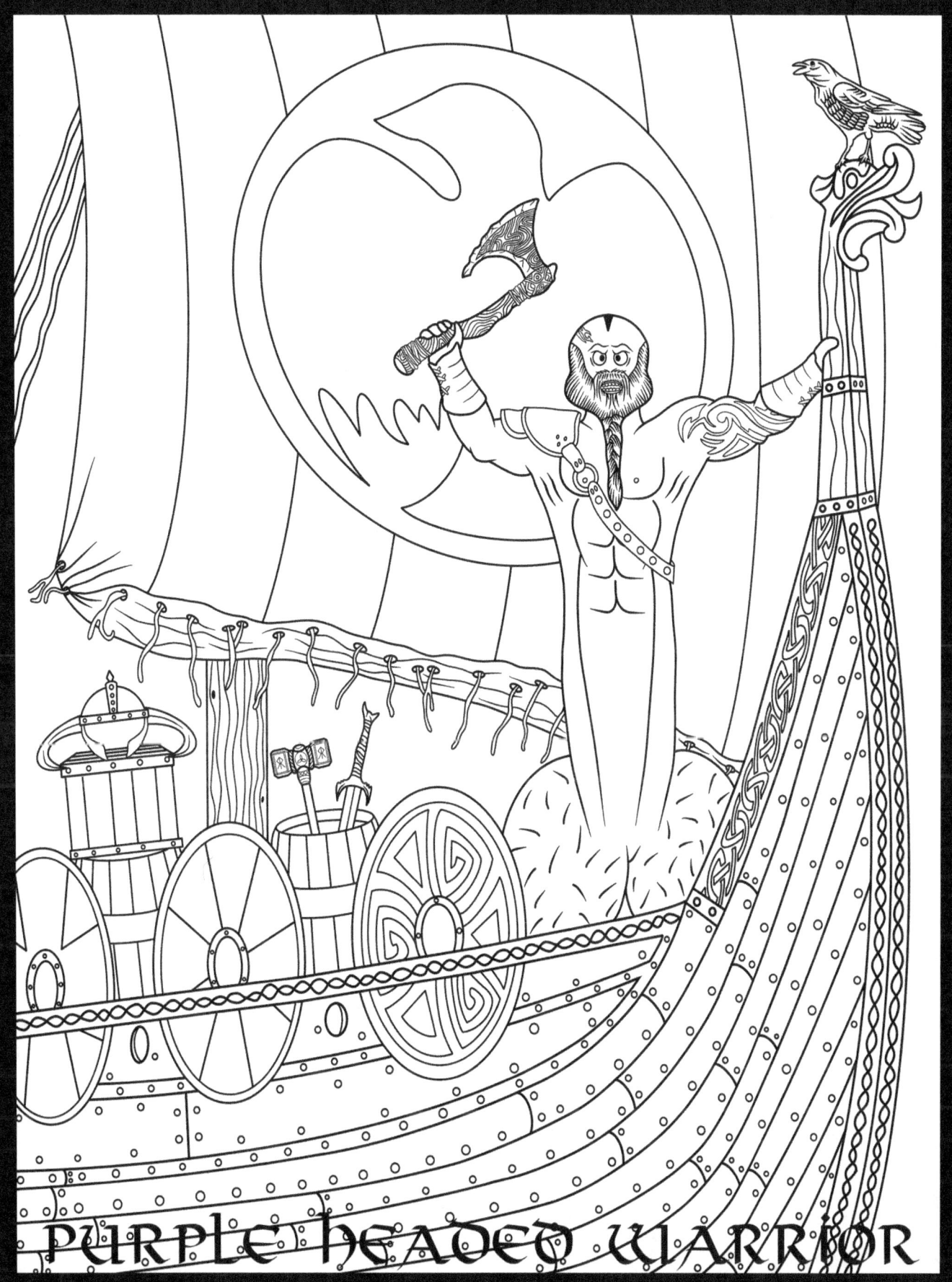

PURPLE HEADED WARRIOR

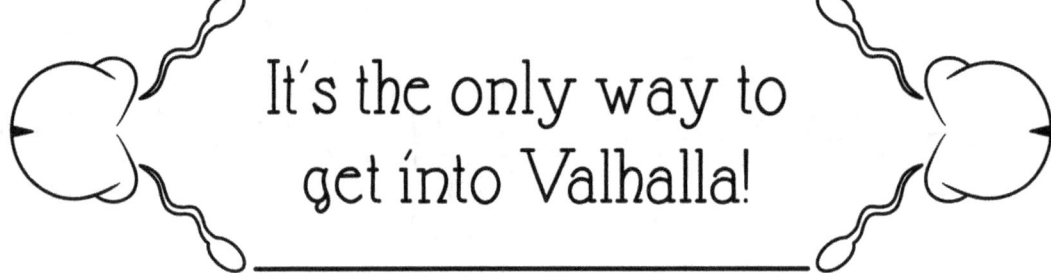

It's the only way to
get into Valhalla!

THE VEIN CANE

Pimps don't fall in love!

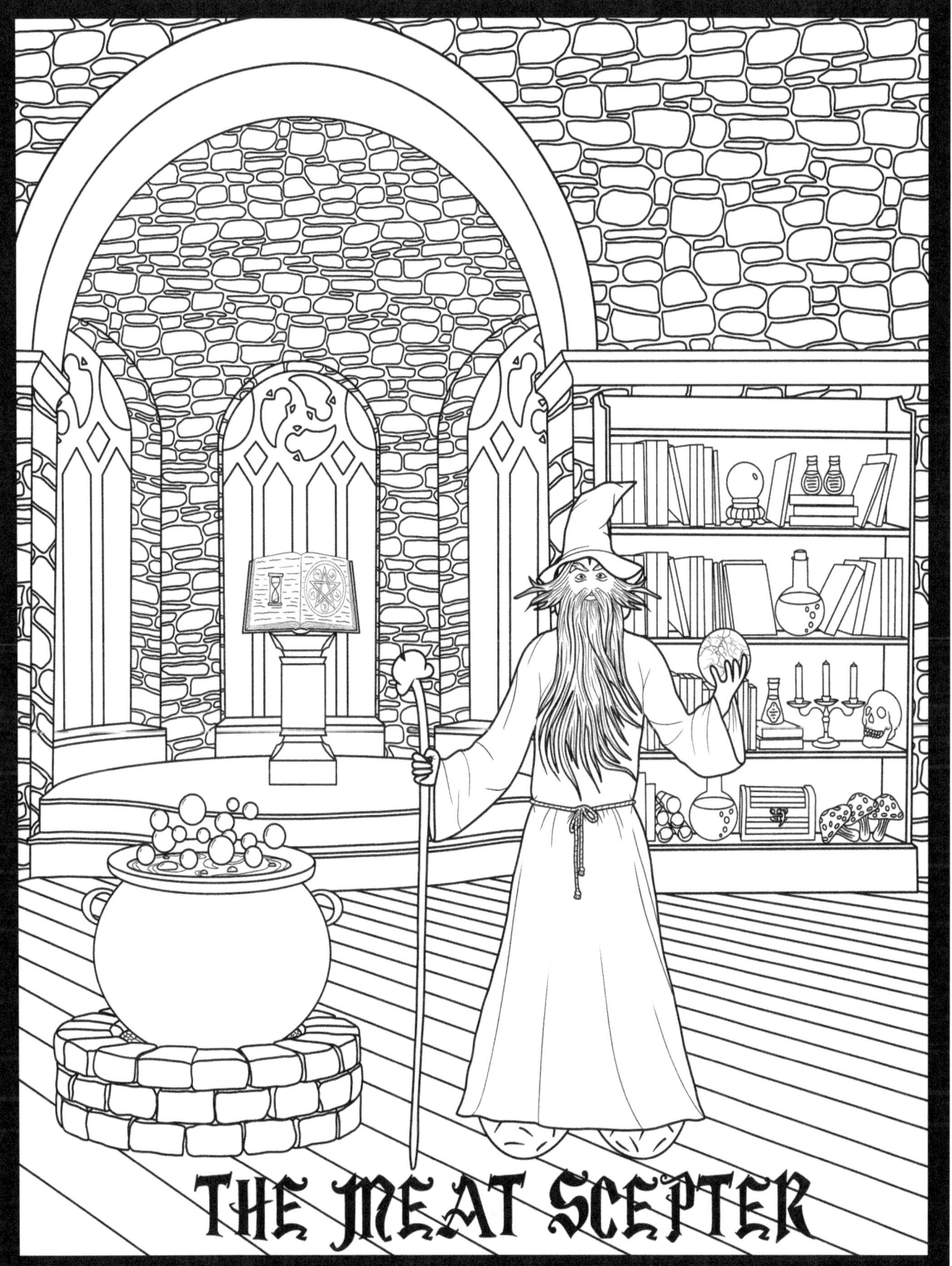

THE MEAT SCEPTER

Making that magic!

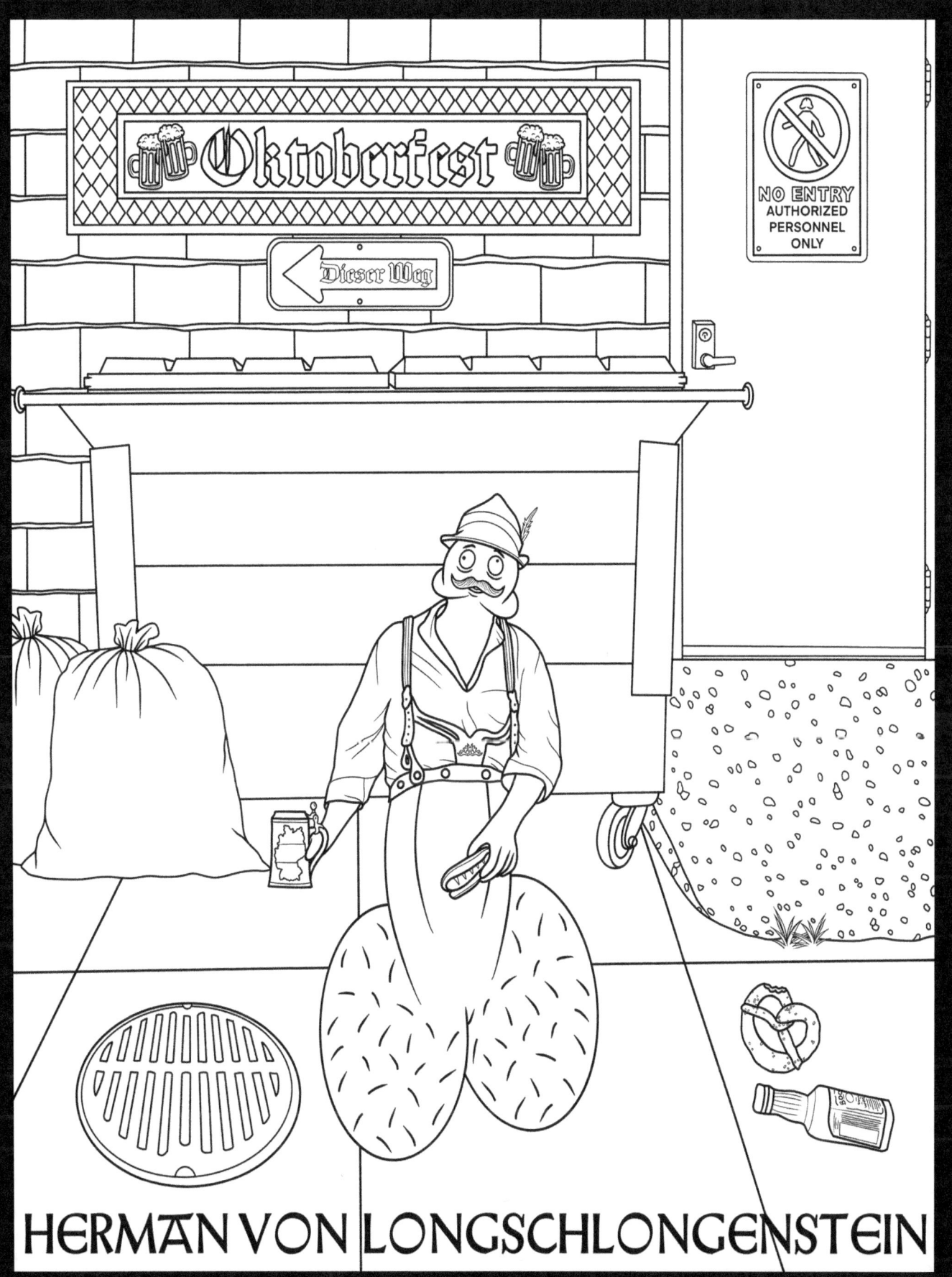

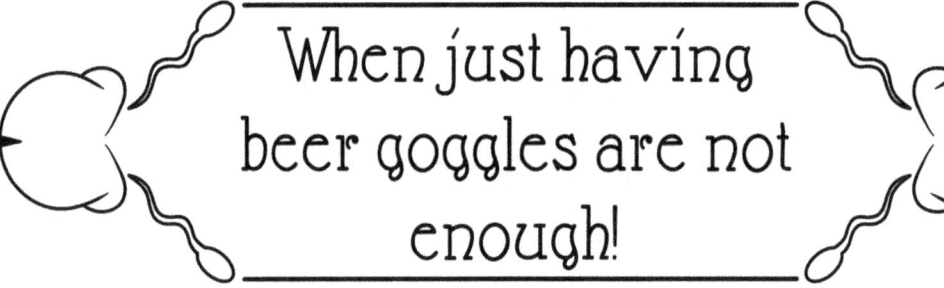

When just having
beer goggles are not
enough!

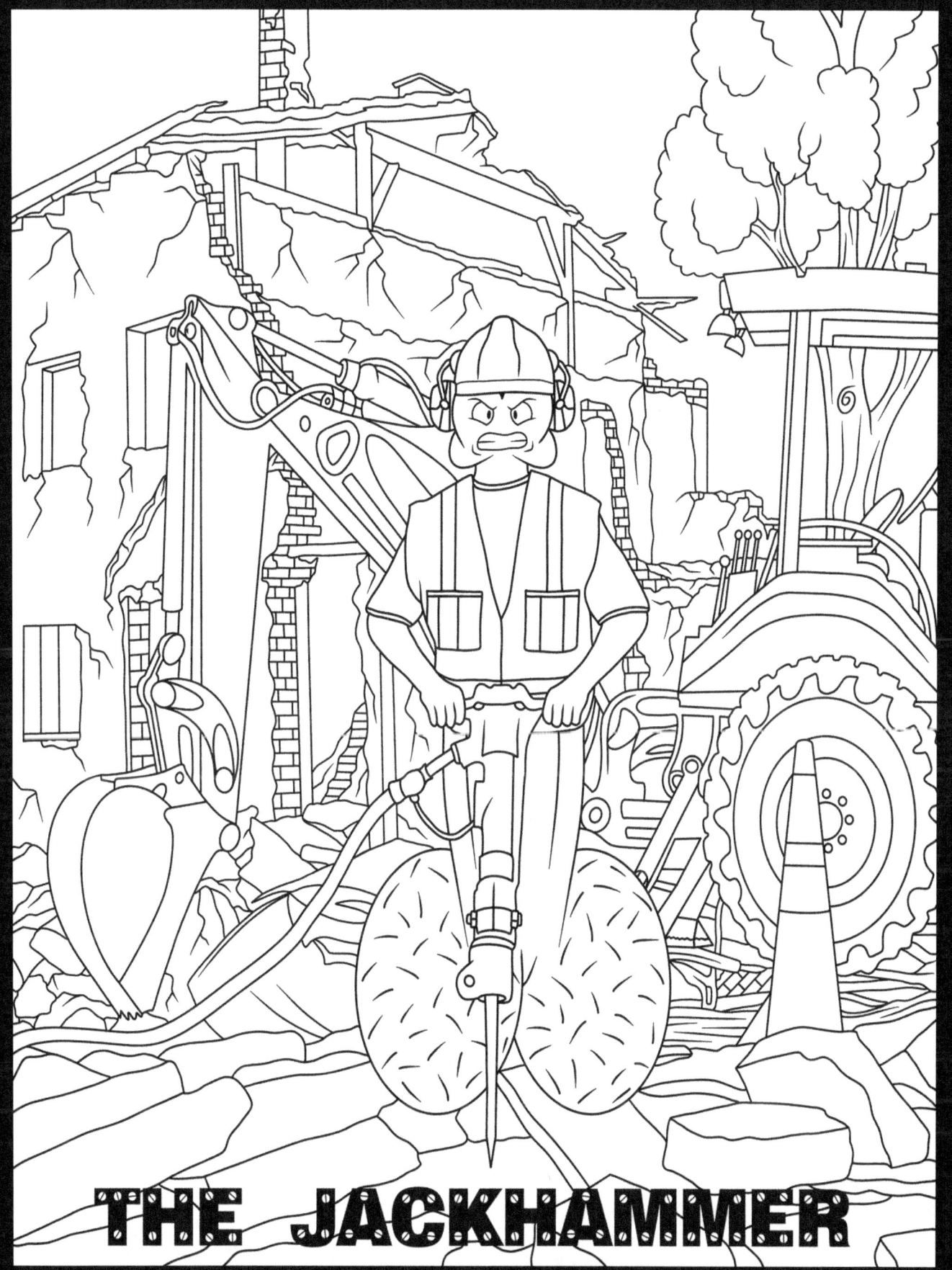

Hammering holes
across the city!

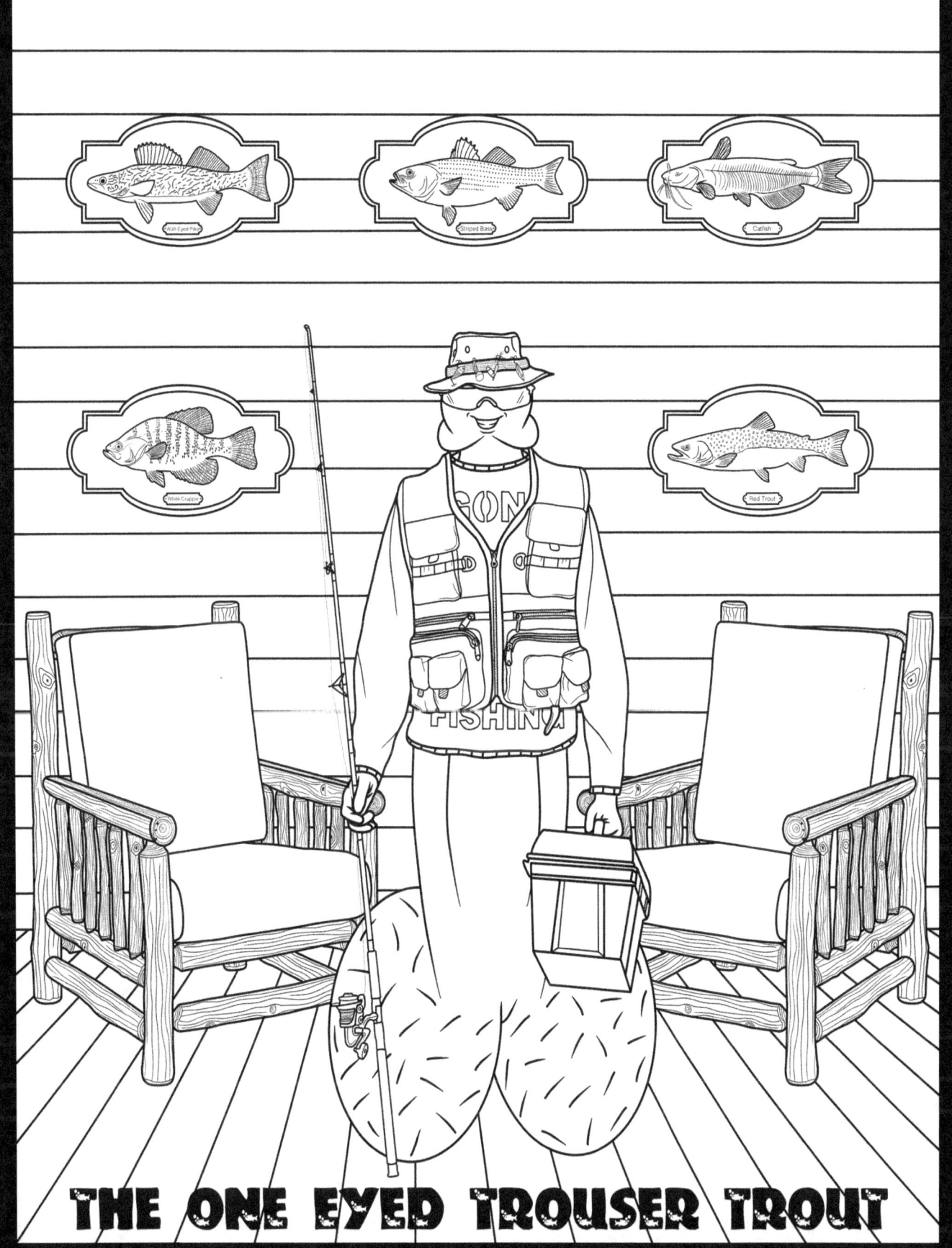

THE ONE EYED TROUSER TROUT

When you need to put
the outdoorsman in her!

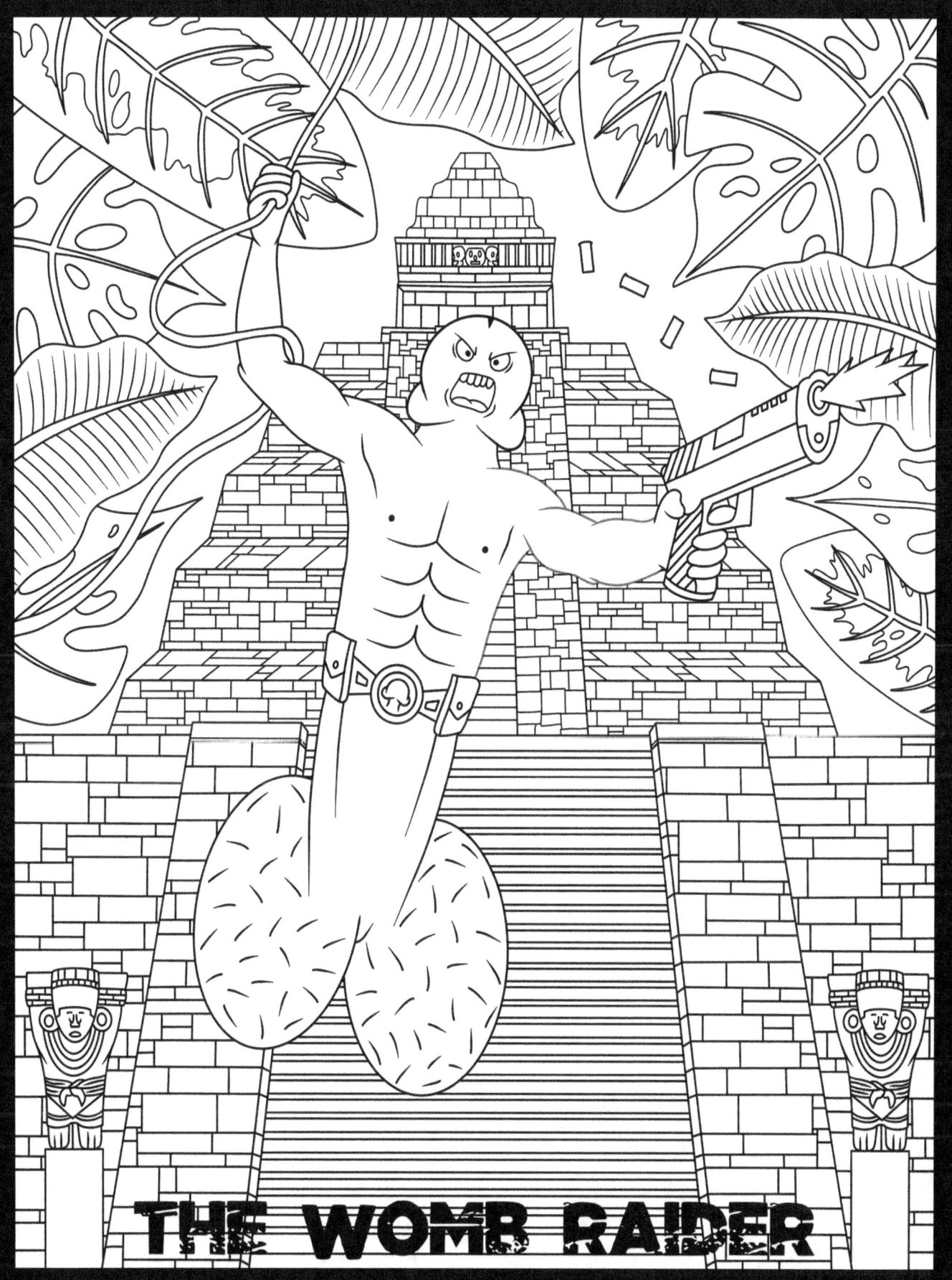

When invading caves
in games is not enough!

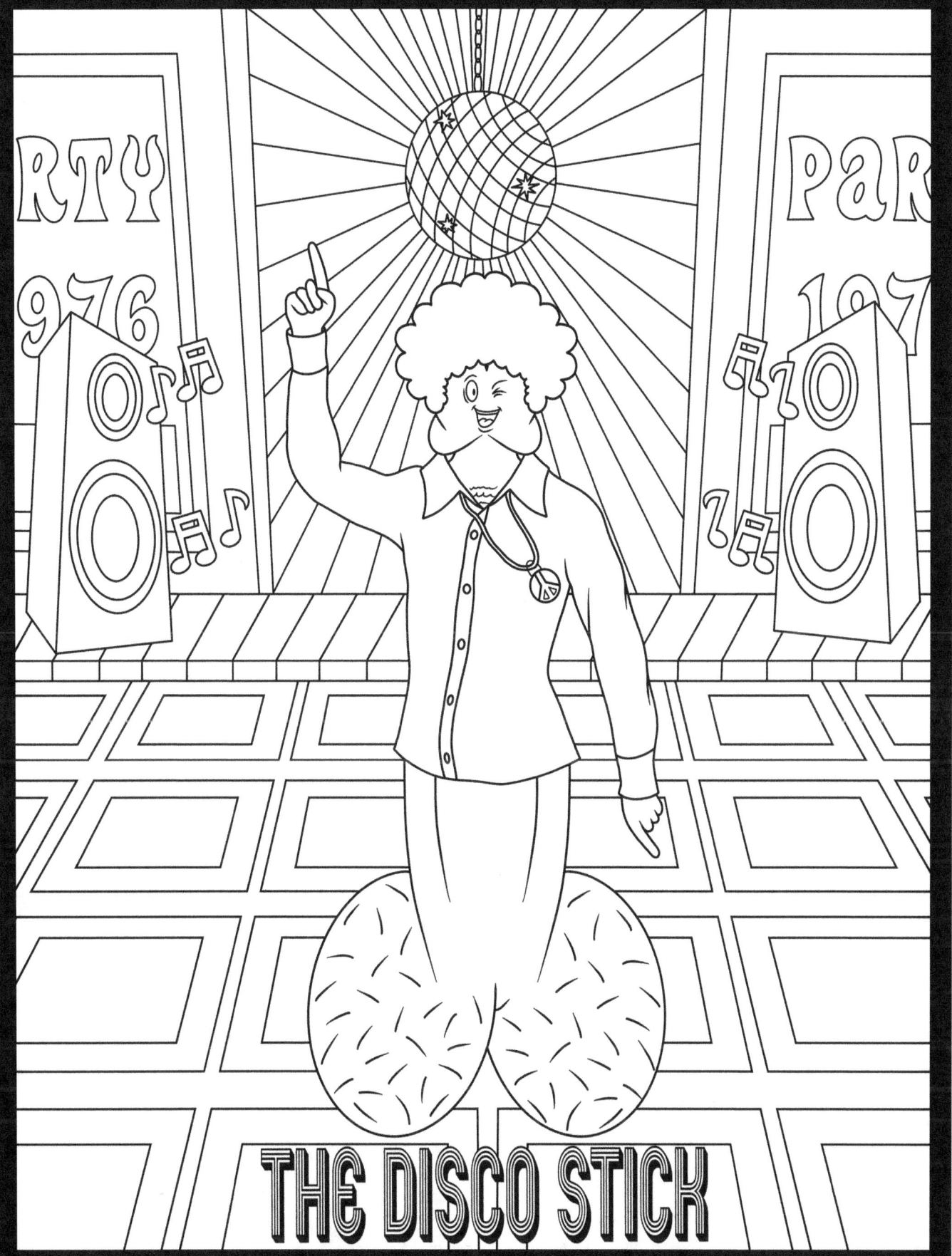

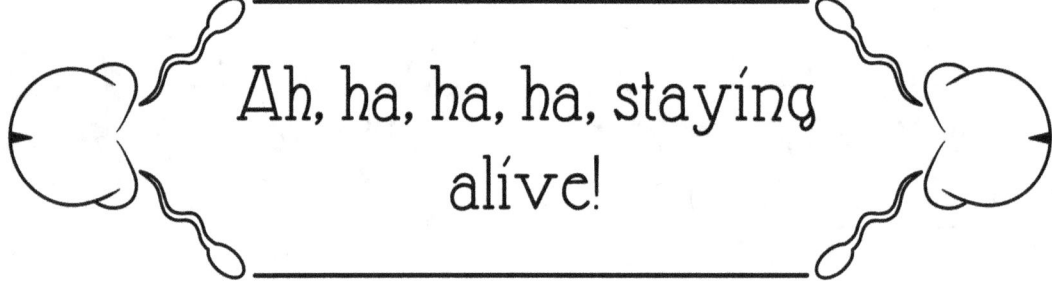

Ah, ha, ha, ha, staying alive!

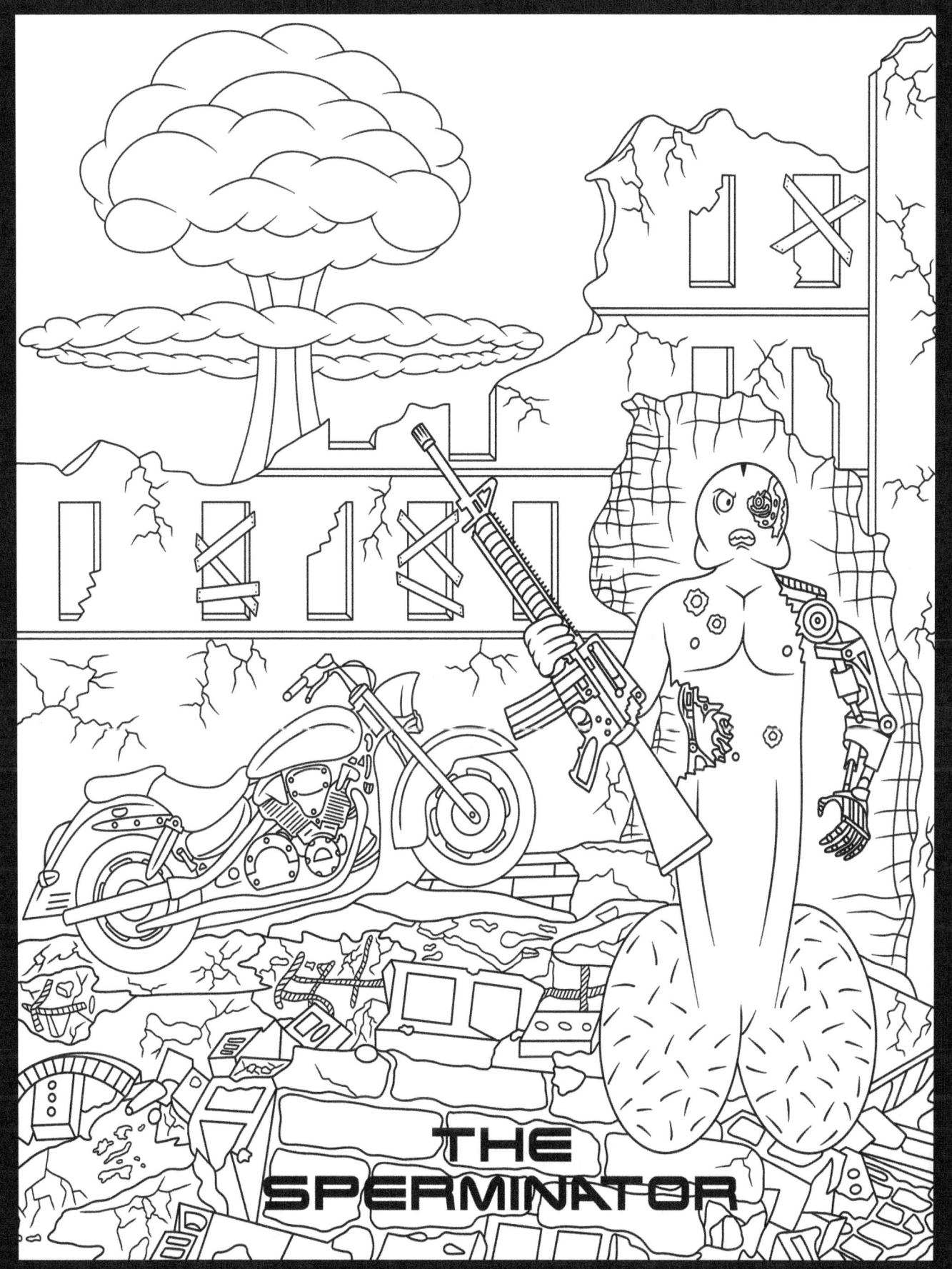

You know he's
coming back!

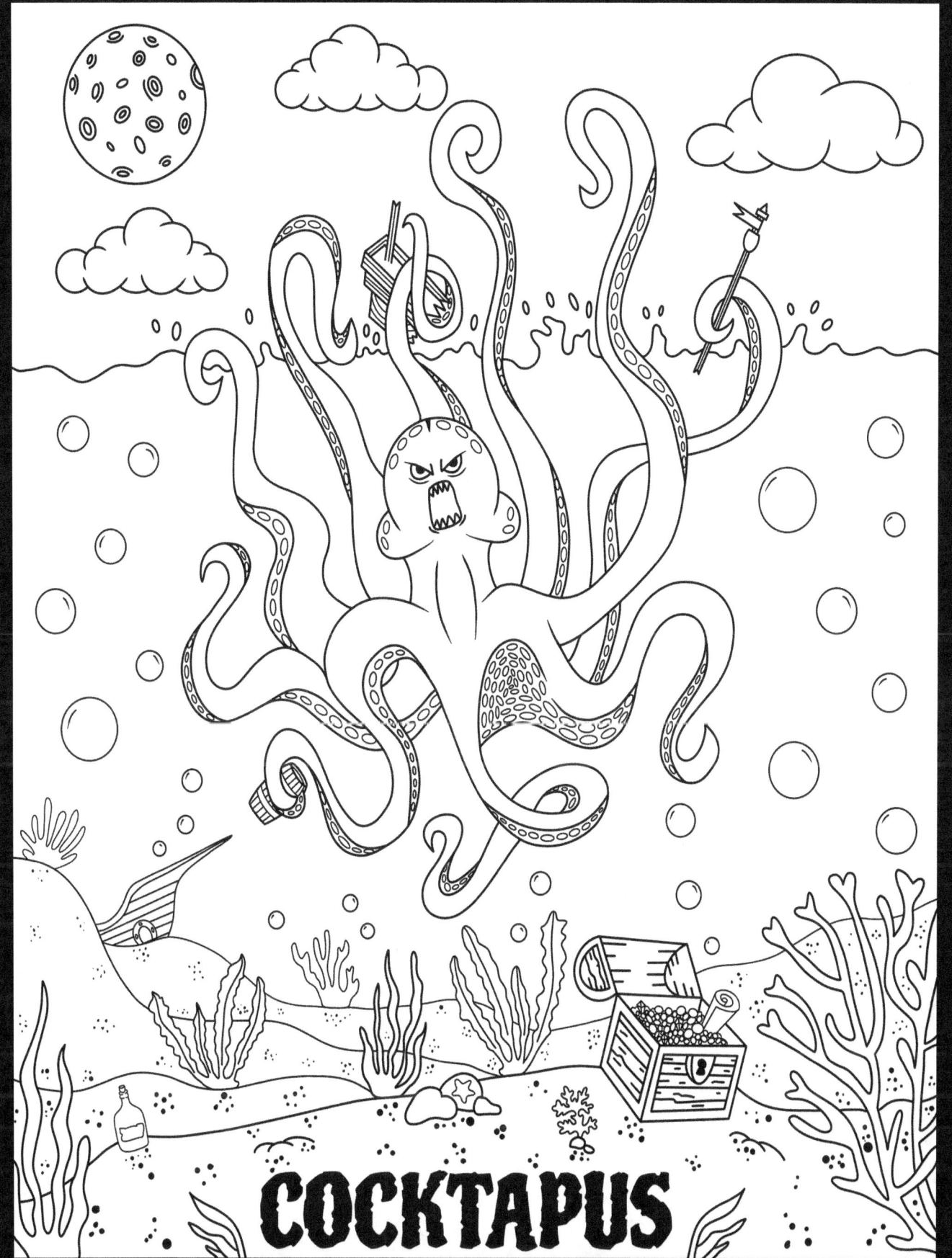

COCKTAPUS

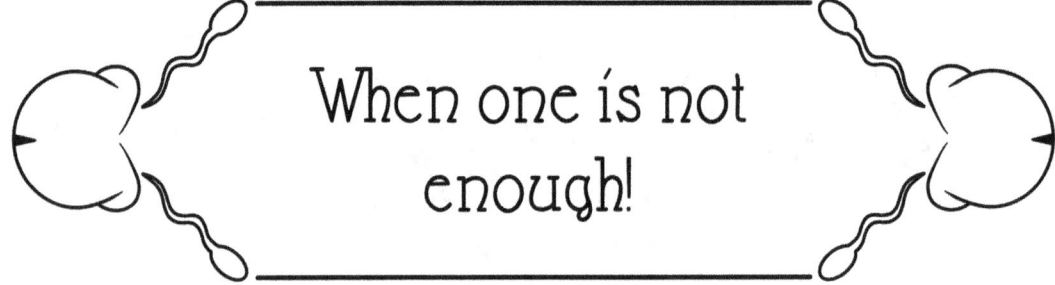

When one is not
enough!

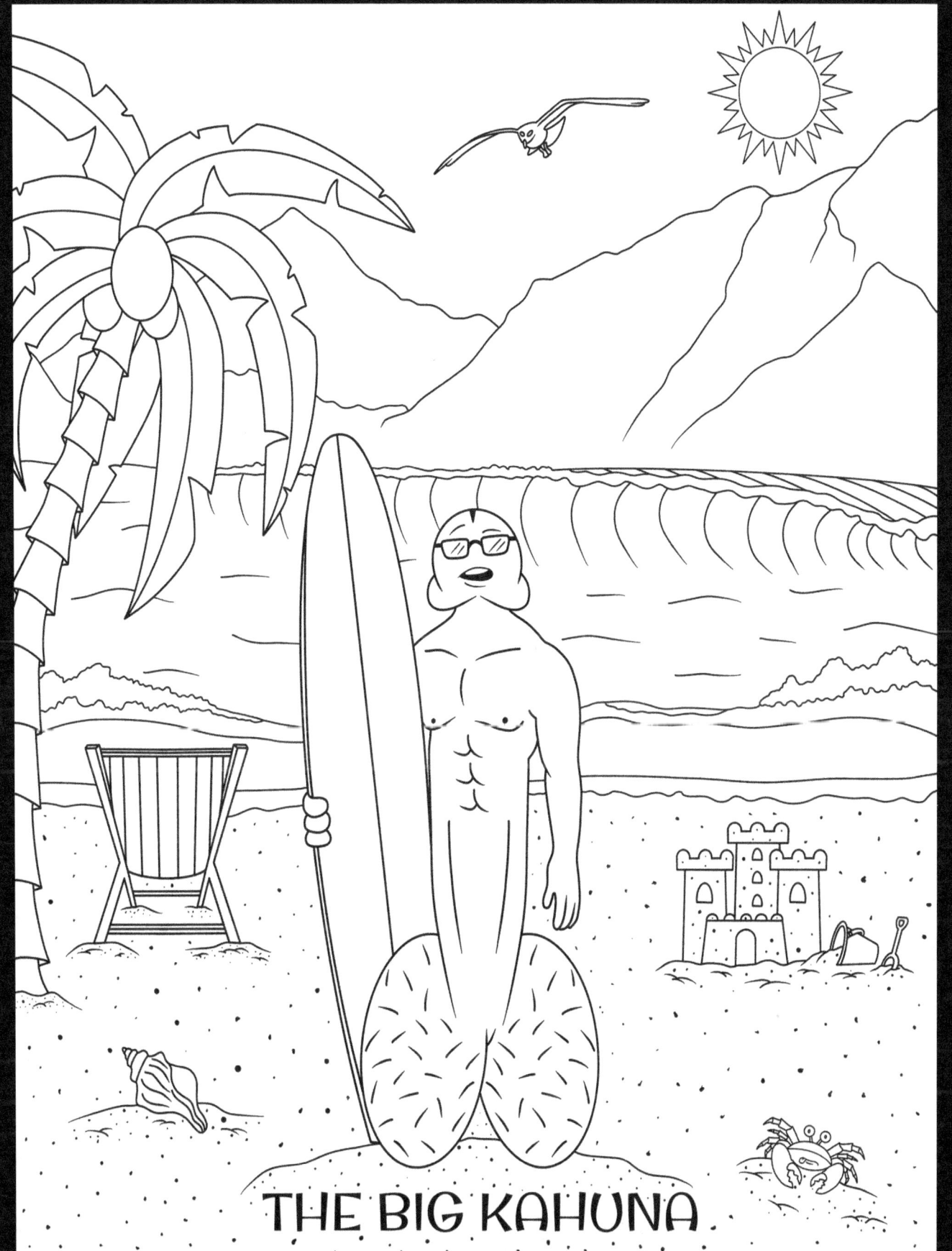

THE BIG KAHUNA

When you need to do
more than ride the wave!

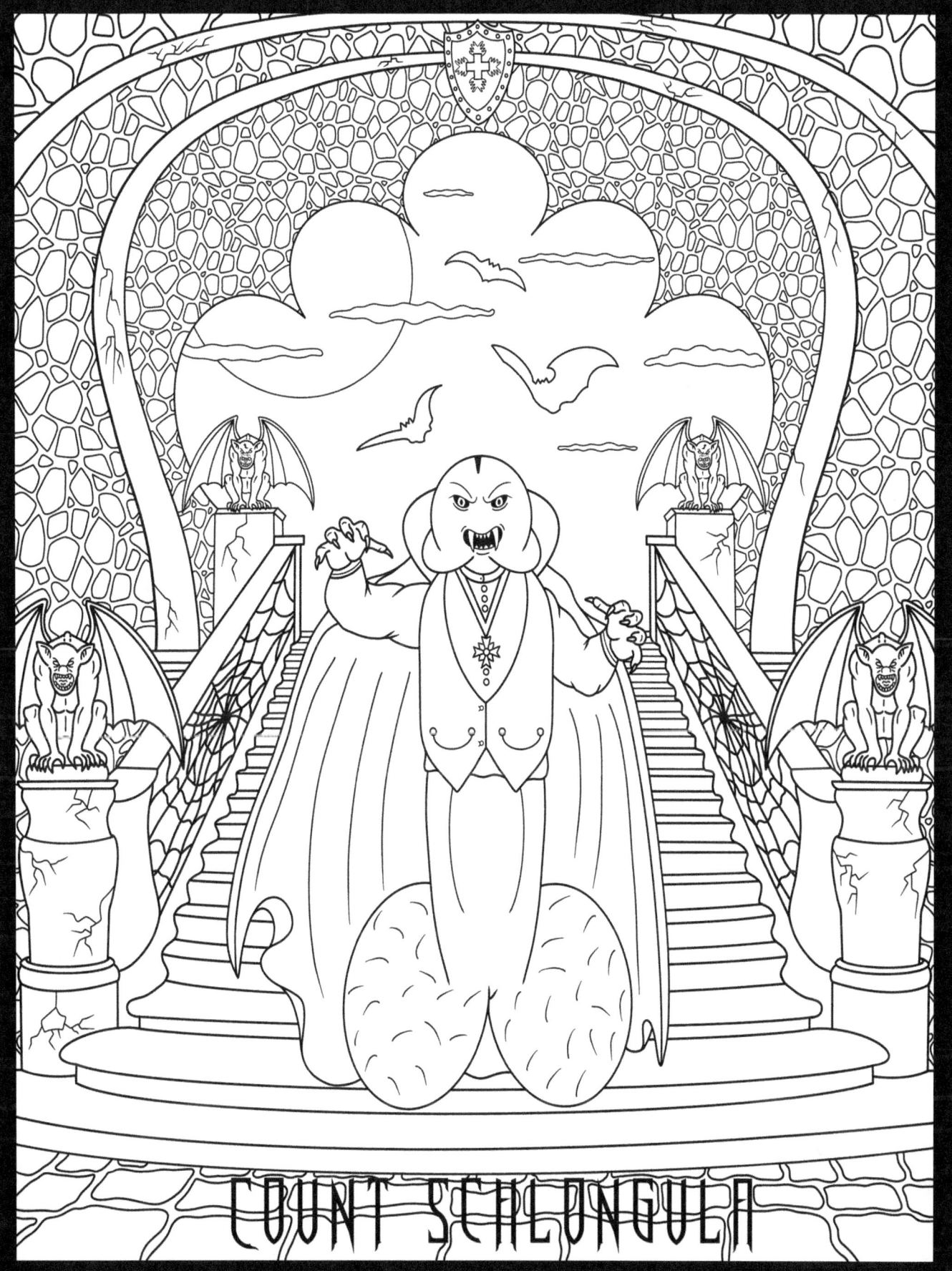

He does the biting,
you do the sucking!

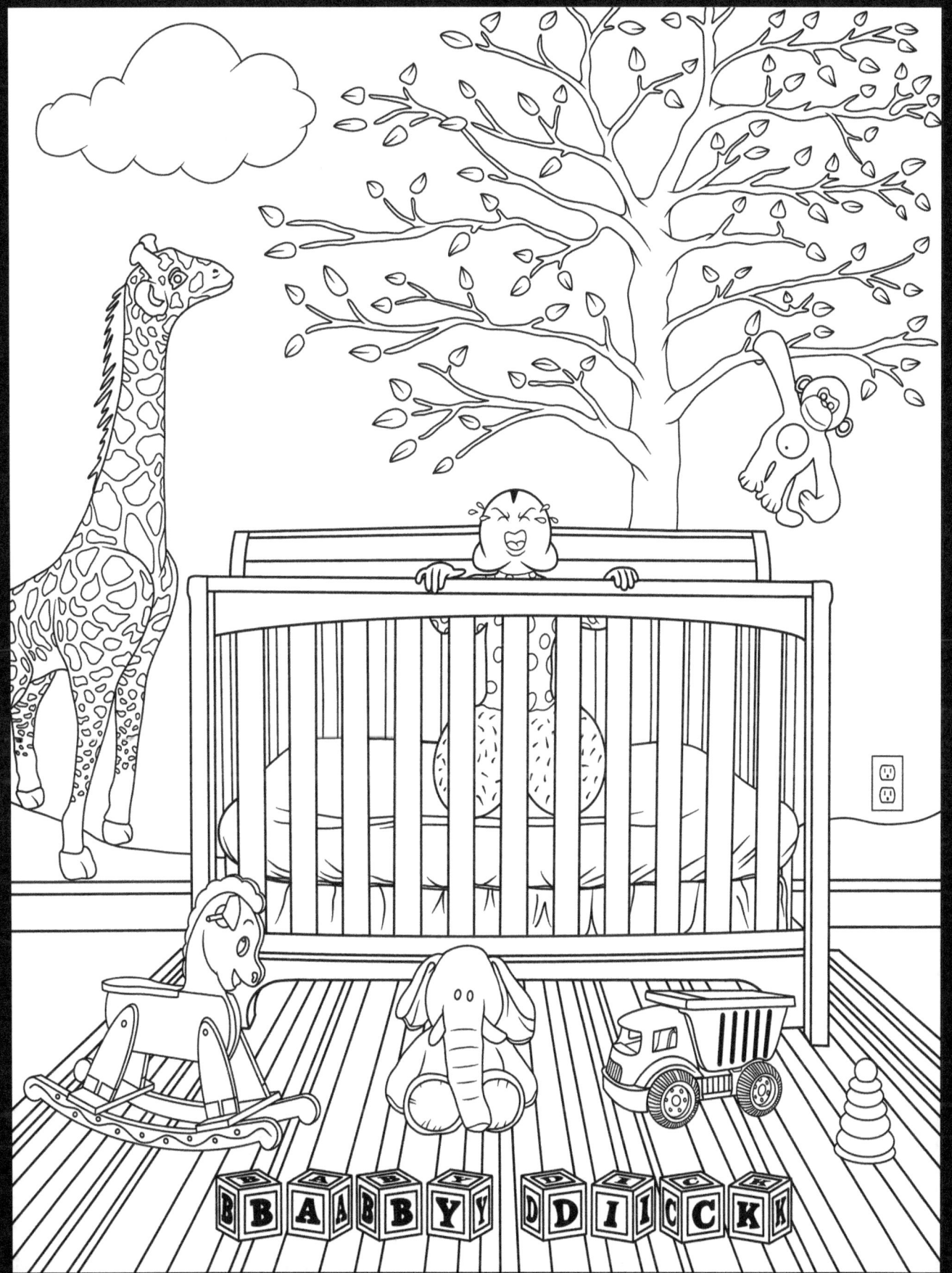

When all you have is
a big heart!

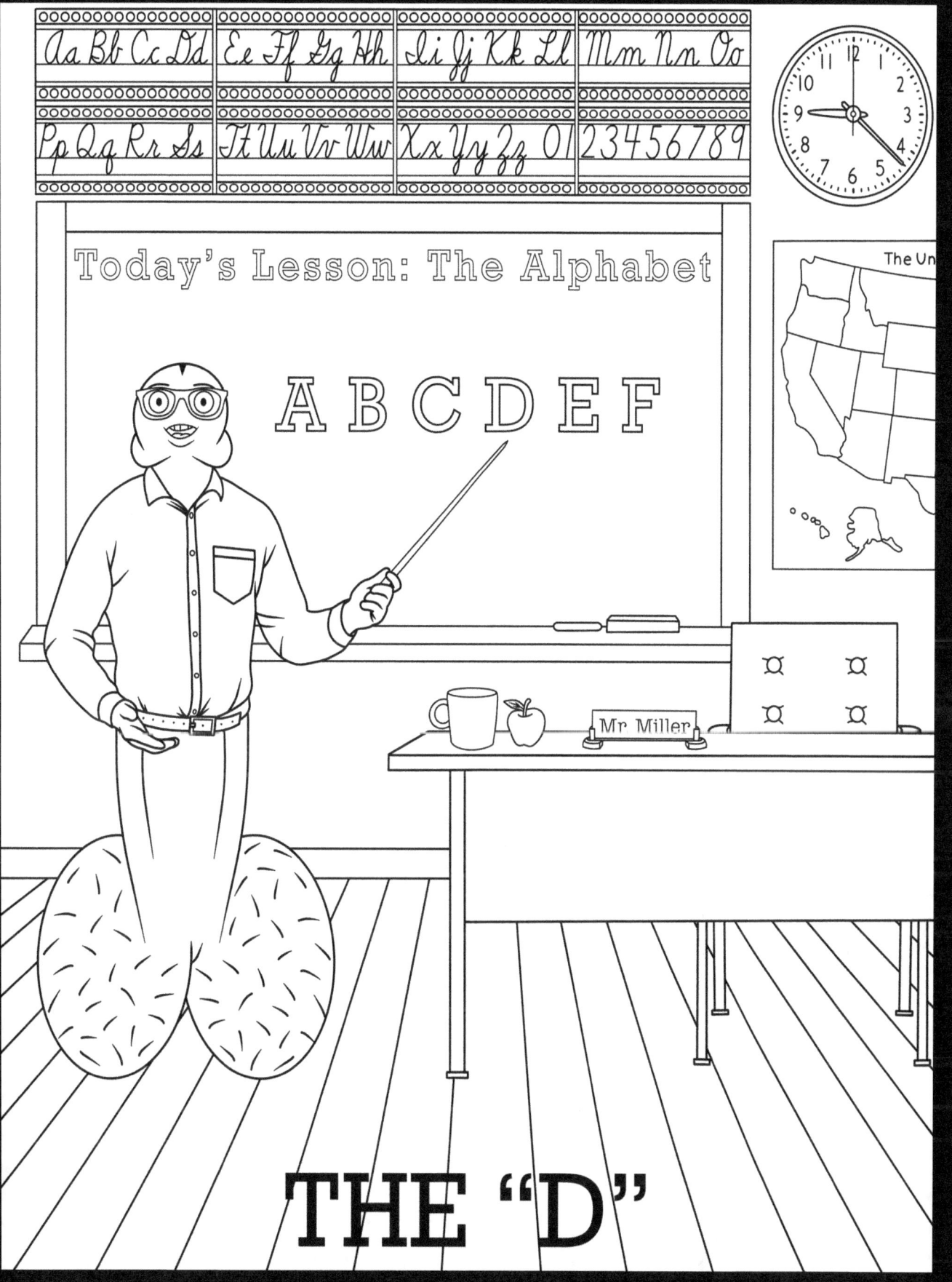

When you need to put
the "D" in detention!

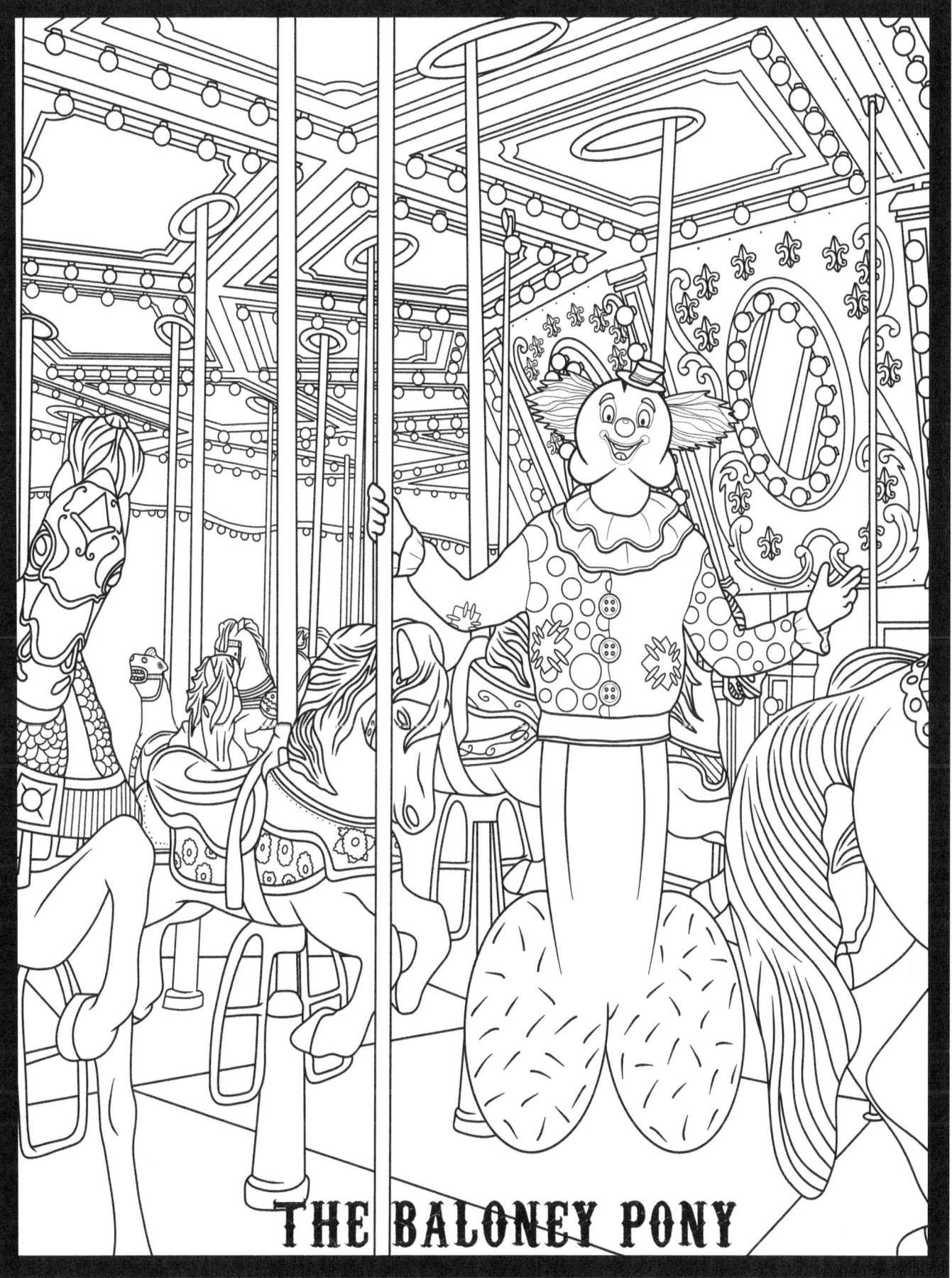

THE BALONEY PONY

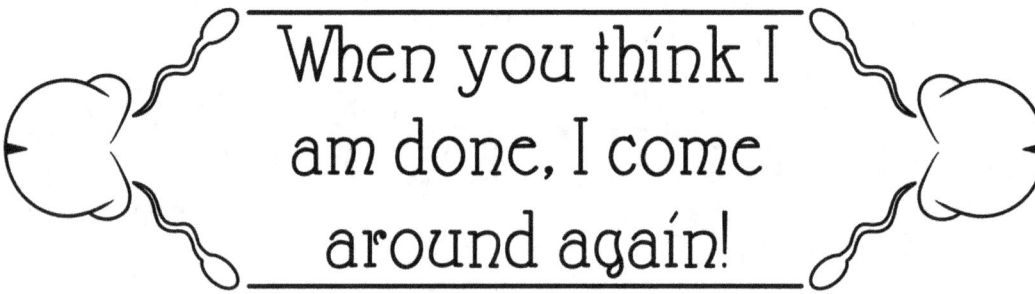

When you think I
am done, I come
around again!

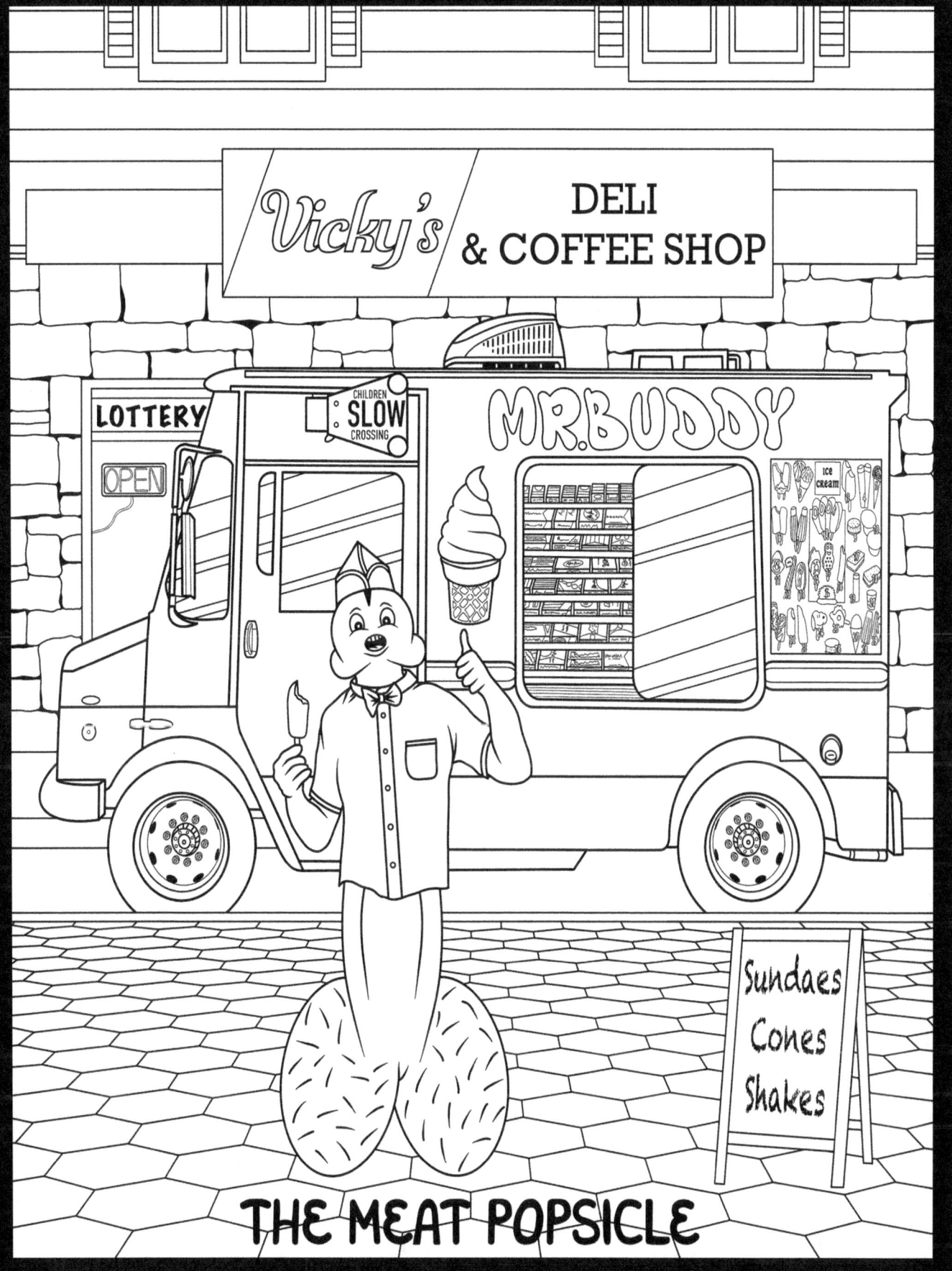

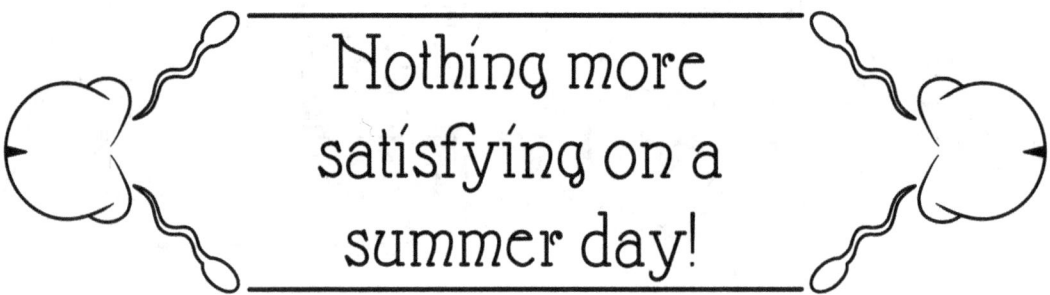

Nothing more
satisfying on a
summer day!

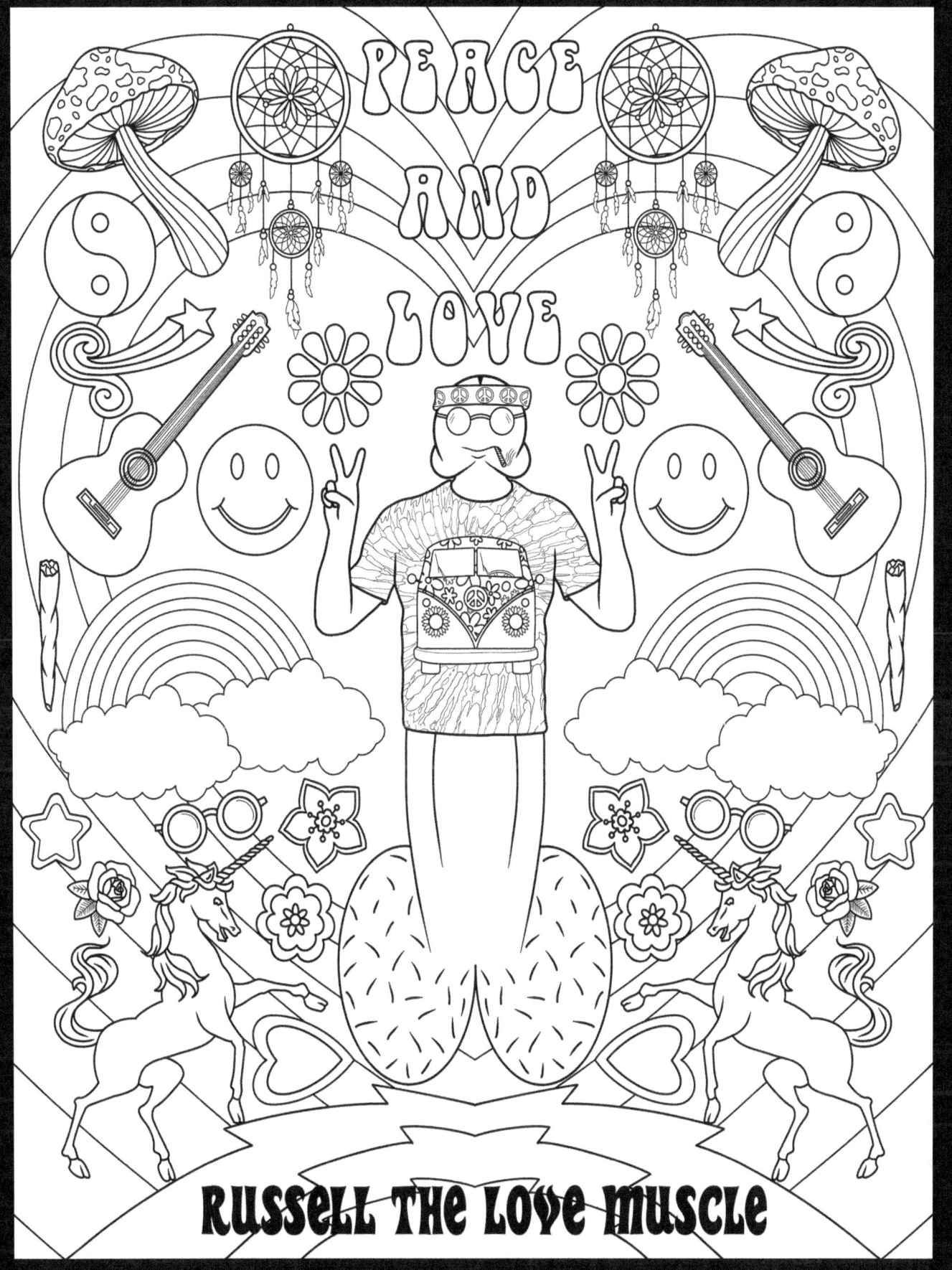

Make love,
not war!

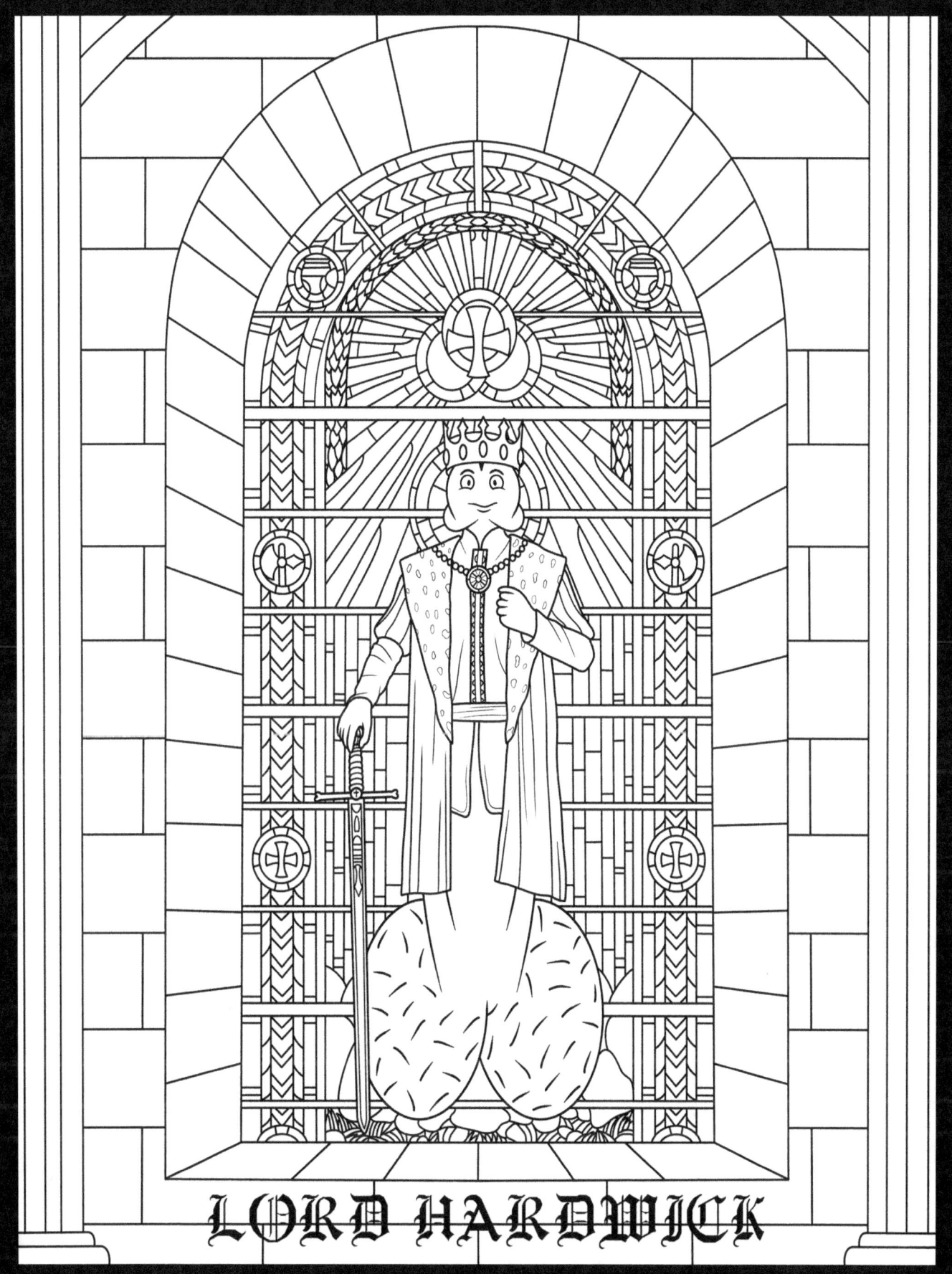

LORD HARDWICK

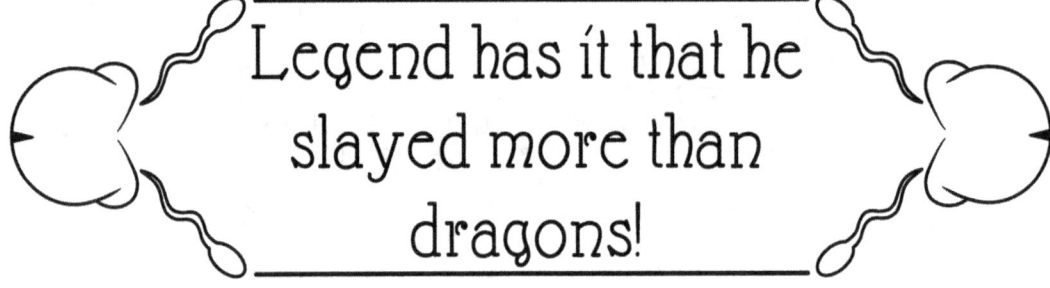

Legend has it that he slayed more than dragons!

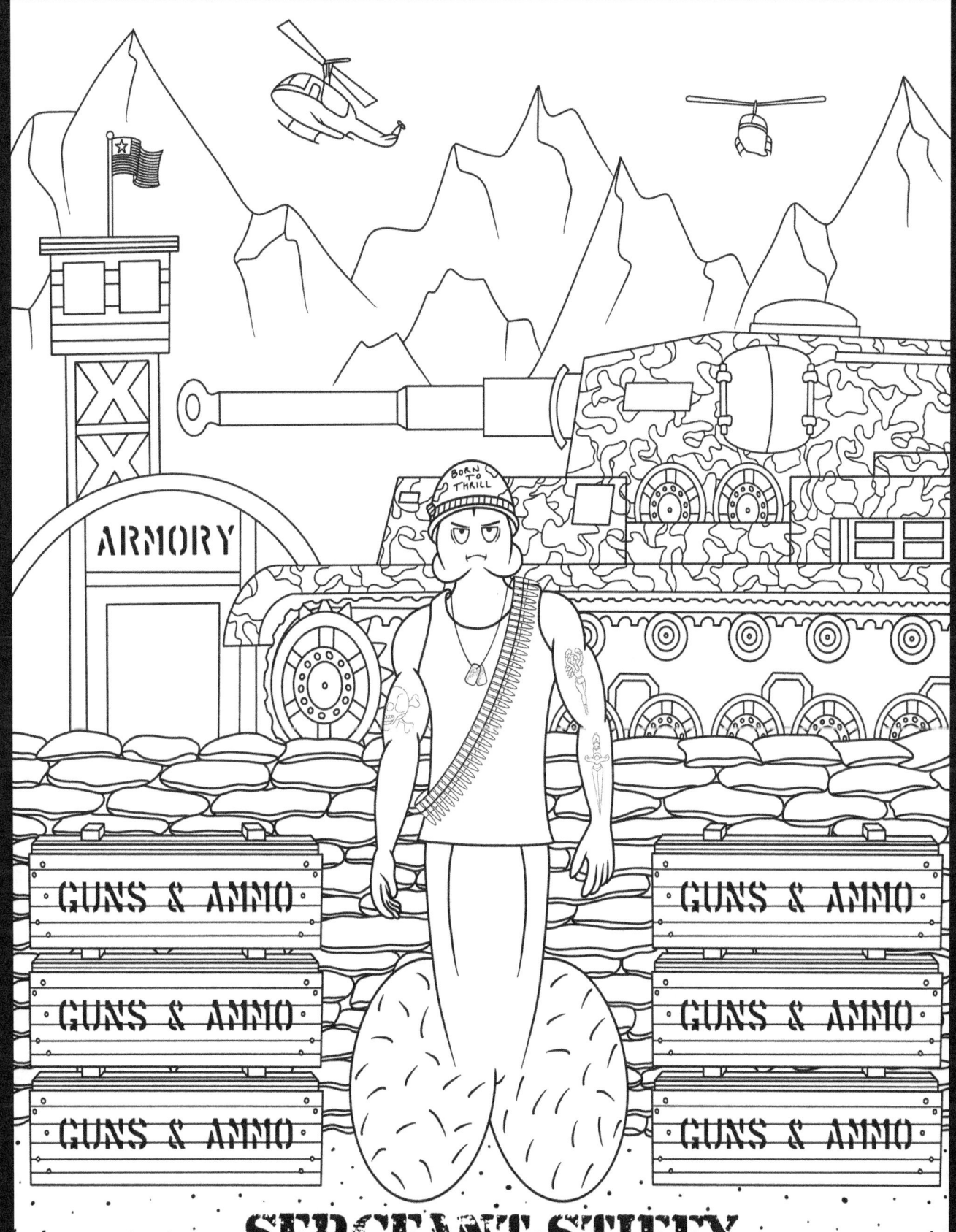

This is my rifle, this is
my gun, both are for fun!

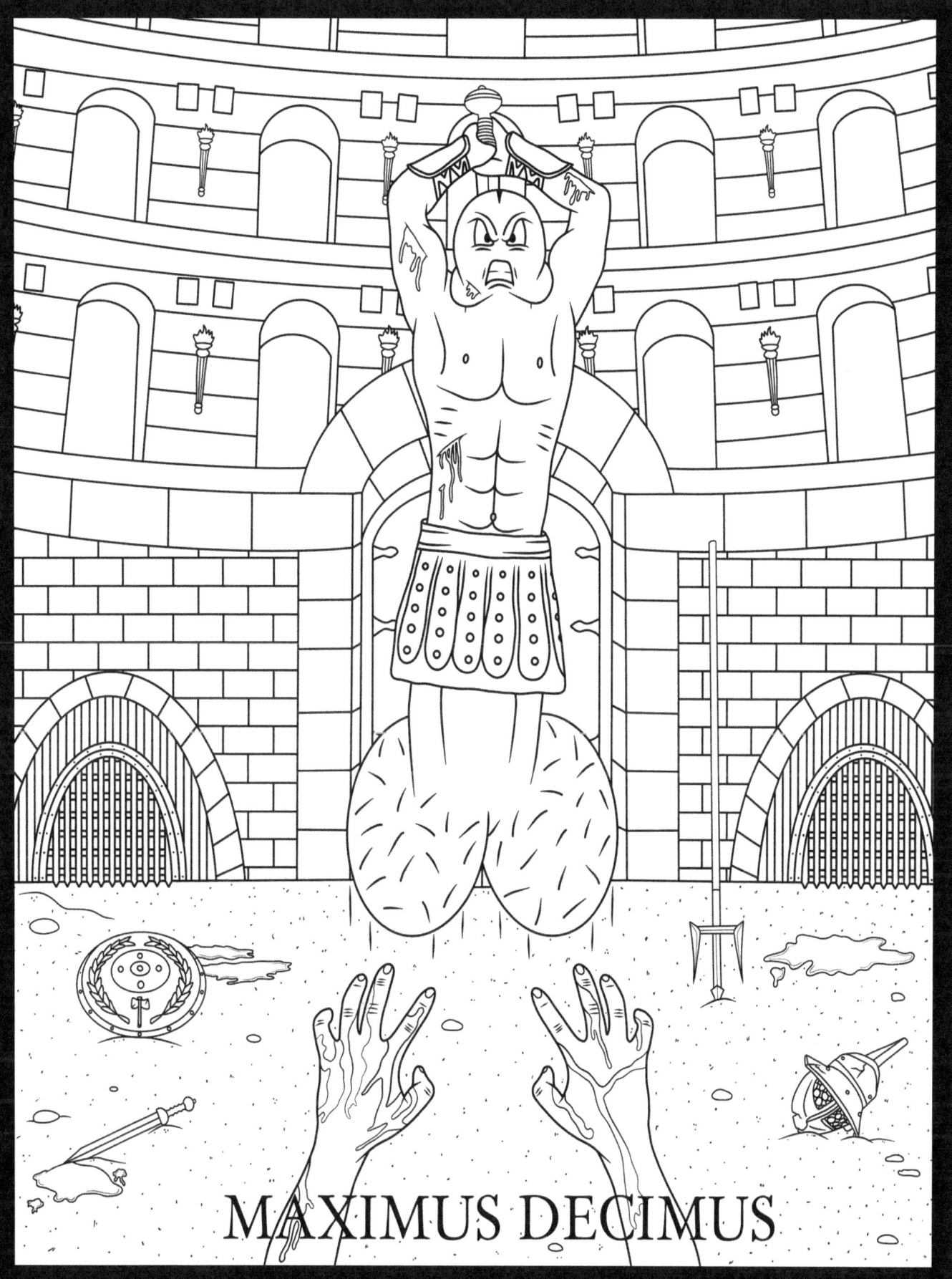

Are you not
entertained?

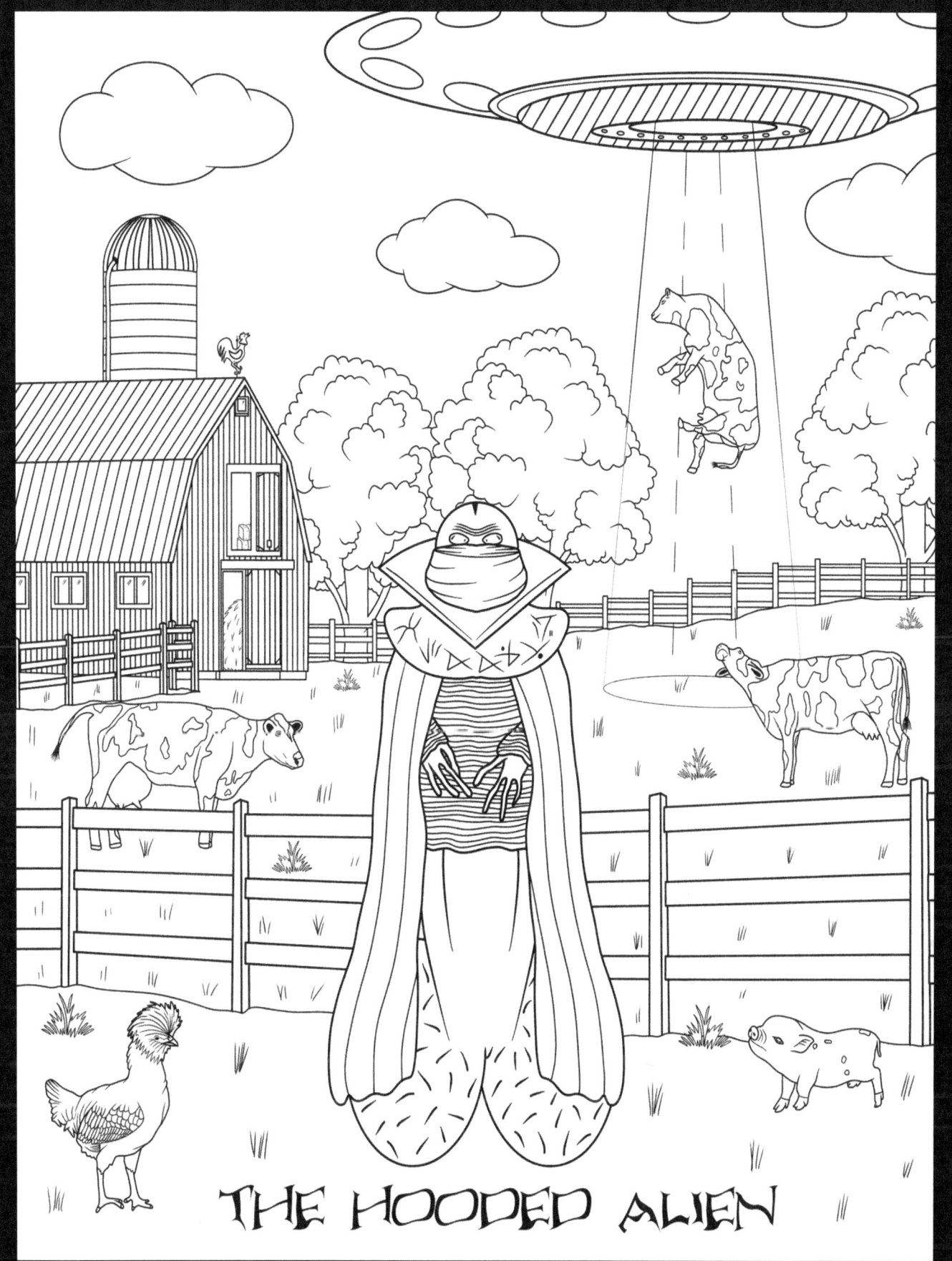

THE HOODED ALIEN

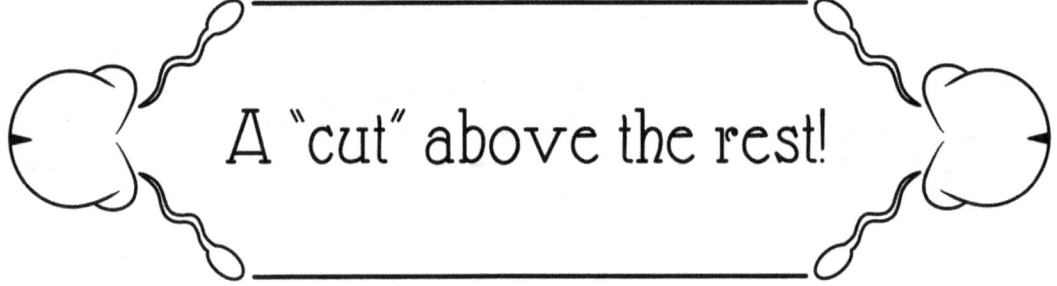

A "cut" above the rest!

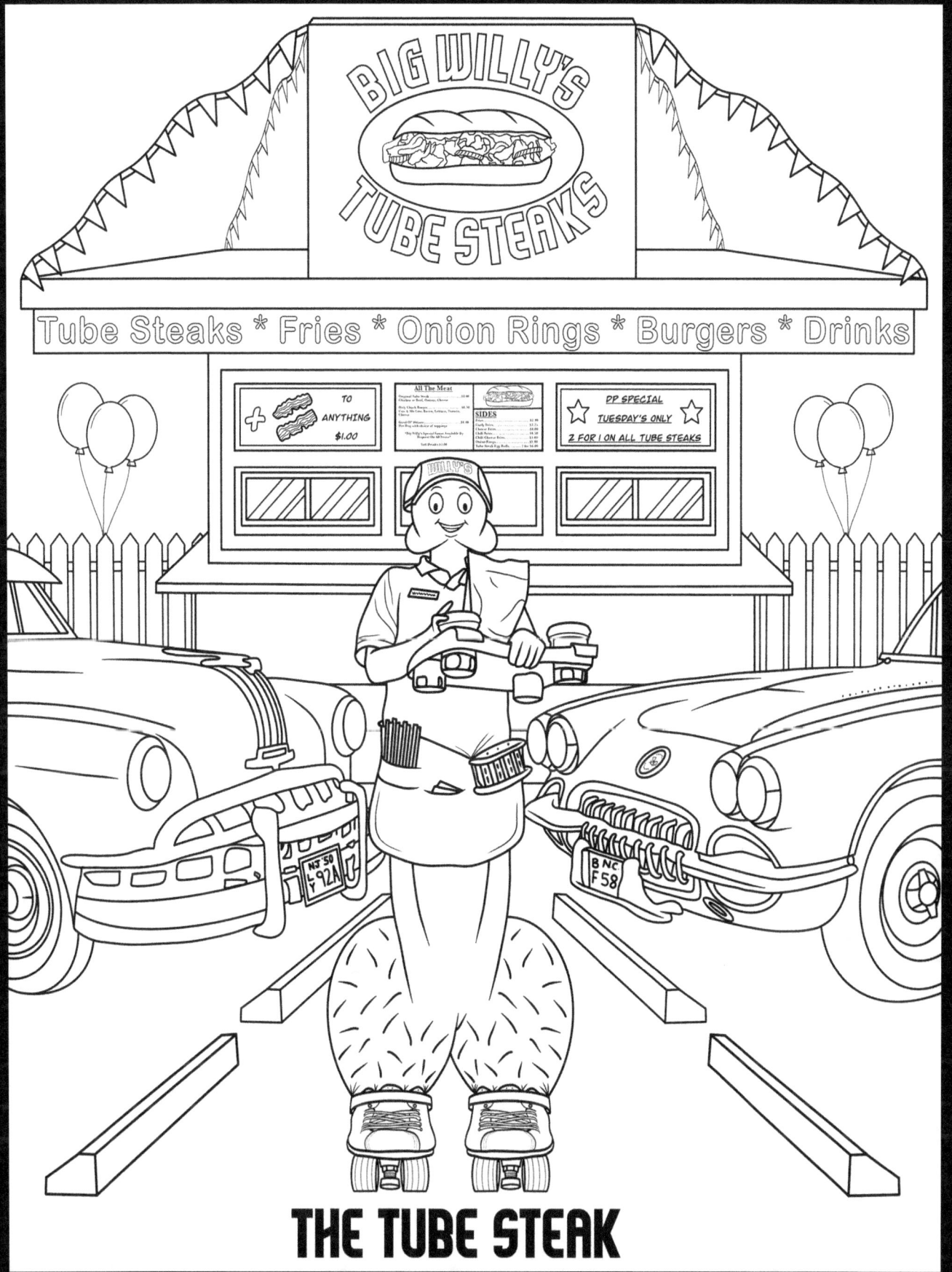

THE TUBE STEAK

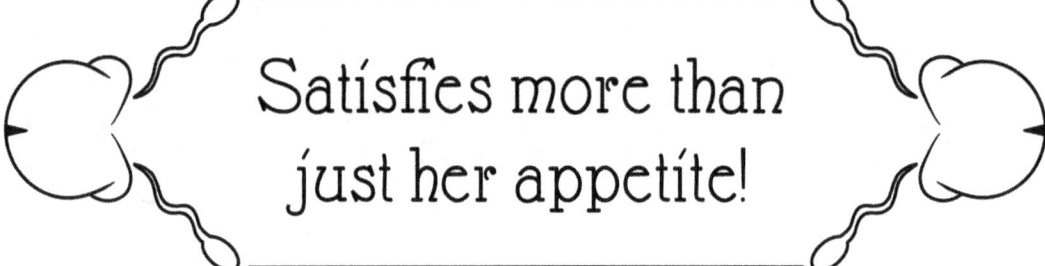

Satisfies more than
just her appetite!

www.ingramcontent.com/pod-product-compliance
Lightning Source LLC
Chambersburg PA
CBHW080958220526
45467CB00008B/2609